The Pelican Guide to
VIRGINIA

SHIRLEY MORRIS

A FIREBIRD PRESS BOOK

PELICAN PUBLISHING COMPANY
Gretna 1998

First edition, 1981
Second edition, 1990

Library of Congress Cataloging in Publication Data

Morris, Shirley.
  The Pelican guide to Virginia / by Shirley Morris. — 2nd ed.
    p. cm.
  Includes index.
  ISBN 0-88289-732-2
  1. Virginia—Description and travel—1981 —Guide-books.
  I. Title.
F224.3.M67 1989
917.5504'43—dc20
                                       89-8701
                                           CIP

*To the Lord, Who leadeth me
in the paths of righteousness.*

*Information in this guidebook is based on authoritative data available at the time
of printing. Prices and hours of operation of businesses listed are subject to change
without notice. Readers are asked to take this into account when consulting this
guide.*

Photographs courtesy of Virginia Division of Tourism

Manufactured in the United States of America
Published by Pelican Publishing Company, Inc.
1000 Burmaster Street, Gretna, Louisiana 70053

Contents

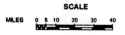
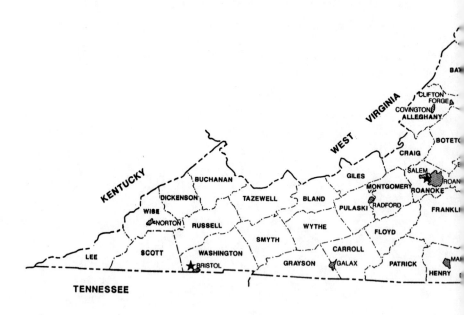

Map courtesy of Virginia Department of Transportation

DO YOURSELF A FAVOR . . .

. . . and come to Virginia, because we've got it all. Delightful country inns. Picturesque villages and bustling cities. White, sandy beaches. Spectacular caverns. Camping from the mountains to the sea. Golfing, skiing, swimming, and saltwater sport fishing.

And if history is what you're looking for, then look no further. You can walk in Washington's footsteps at Mount Vernon, America's most historic house. Stroll along quiet lanes in the restored village of Appomattox, where Lee surrendered to Grant. Visit a 15th-century English Tudor mansion where King Charles I attended a wedding. Stay at an old inn where rooms are appointed with canopy beds and fireplaces. Dine on food prepared from 200-year-old recipes. Stand at Jamestown, the site of our nation's beginnings. And visit Yorktown, where America won her independence.

Then step into the twentieth century at N.A.S.A.'s Langley Research Center, where you can see David Scott's space suit and a real moon rock. Spend a fun-filled day at a 300-acre replica of the Old Country of Europe, or at a $50-million giant entertainment complex where you can take a monorail ride through a jungle inhabited by wild animals. Drift among cool waterways in the world's largest azalea and camellia garden. Sit under the stars or in an open-sided, Oregon red cedar theatre and enjoy performances by renowned artists of dance, jazz, opera, and folk music.

Enjoy us—our history and our heritage, our unforgettable scenery, fun, and excitement—and most of all, the warm and friendly people of Virginia, who are waiting to make this your best vacation ever!

**And now,
Welcome to Virginia!**

Alphabetical Listing of Attractions

Abingdon

Barter Theatre (Main Street, on U.S. 11 and I-81). This theatre was founded in 1932 as a haven for out-of-work Broadway performers during the Great Depression, with homemade jams and jellies and fresh garden produce bartered for the price of admission. In 1946 it became the first state theatre in the nation, and, except for New York, has maintained the largest professional company in continuous operation. Many renowned figures in the entertainment world today—including Gregory Peck, Ernest Borgnine, and Patricia Neal—received their start here. The 380-seat air-conditioned theatre offers professional productions, and across the street is the Playhouse, where a flexible stage provides a suitable atmosphere for contemporary and experimental drama. The Barter Box Office also handles reservations for the Playhouse.

Theatregoers can enjoy fine restaurant or buffet dining at the Martha Washington Inn, across the street from the Barter Theatre.

Performances nightly, except Mondays, matinees Wednesdays, Thursdays, Saturdays, and Sundays, April through October. Children's matinees mid-June, July, and August. All seats reserved. For schedules and reservations, write to the

Barter Theatre, P.O. Box 867, Abingdon, VA 24210, or phone (703) 628-3991, toll free in Virginia 1-800-572-2081. Box office open daily, Monday 10 to 5, Tuesday through Saturday 10 A.M. to 8 P.M., and Sunday 4 to 10 P.M.

Grayson Highlands State Park (35 miles southeast of Abingdon on U.S. 58). A Visitor Center has displays of pioneer life and special programs. The park offers hiking, horseback riding, camping, and picnicking. Park entrance fee. Open April through October. For more information phone (703) 579-7092.

White's Mill (3.5 miles north of Abingdon on VA 692, on White's Mill Road). Visitors can watch an old gristmill in operation.

Afton Mountain

Blue Ridge Parkway (begins at Rockfish Gap near Afton, VA, the southern terminus of the Skyline Drive; *see* Shenandoah National Park). Extending for 469 miles through the Southern Appalachian Mountains at an average elevation of 3,000 feet, this toll-free parkway ribbons through the Shenandoah National Park in Virginia to the Great Smoky Mountains National Park in North Carolina and Tennessee. Motorists can enjoy leisurely travel (speed limit 45 mph) along this scenic highway which has no commercial vehicles, bypasses all towns, and has available abundant fuel, food, and lodging. The parkway is splashed with color during the spring season, with flowering dogwood in early May, mountain laurel and azaleas in early June, and rhododendron in late June. From mid-October through November, the brilliant foliage of autumn flames into reds and golds of hickory, maple, and sassafras trees. Highland farms, weathered barns, and miles of split-rail fences lend evidence of the pioneer culture of the Blue Ridge mountain people. Six visitor centers, open May through October, have exhibits of historical interest. Swimming, picnicking, hiking, camping, and fishing areas are available. The parkway stays open all year, but sections of the road may close in icy or snowy weather.

Numbered mileposts indicate stopping sites with special features (southbound):

(Mile 5 to 9.3) **Humpback Rocks.** Mile 5.8—Visitor Center, comfort station, reconstruction of a mountain homestead. Open 9 A.M. to 6 P.M.—Picnic area, comfort station. Mile 8.8—Self-guiding trail from Greenstone Parking Overlook. Stone fences are remnants of walls built in early 1800s to control the wanderings of hogs that foraged for chestnuts and acorns.

(Mile 16, VA 814 to Sherando Lake, 4.5 miles) **U.S. Forest Service Recreation Area.** Swimming, camping, picnicking.

(Mile 29) **Whetstone Ridge.** Ranger's office, restaurant, gas station.

(Mile 34.4) **Yankee Horse Logging Railroad Exhibit.** Waterfall.

(Mile 58 to 63.6) **Otter Creek.** Mile 60.8—Campground, restaurant, gas. Mile 63.1—Otter Lake, fishing, trail. Mile 63.6—**James River Visitor Center** tells the story of the James River and Kanawha Canal. Open dawn to dusk. A footbridge across the James River leads to a restored canal lock.

(Mile 71, Petit Gap, U.S. Forest Service road to Cave Mountain Lake, 7 miles) **Cave Mountain Lake.** Camping, swimming, picnicking.

(Mile 84 to 87) **Peaks of Otter.** Mile 85.6—Lodge, restaurant. Mile 86—Peaks of Otter Visitor Center features exhibits of wildlife, forest plants, and Indian relics. Open 8 A.M. to 8 P.M. Self-guiding trail, restored Johnson Farm, gas, picnic area, road to campgrounds, bus station, hiking trails, ranger's office.

(Mile 154.5) **Smart View.** Picnic area, trails, comfort stations.

(Mile 167 to 174) **Rocky Knob.** Mile 167—Campgrounds. Mile 168—Nature trail. Mile 169—Trails, picnic area. Mile 174—Cabins, ranger's office.

(Mile 176.1) **Mabry Mill.** Visitor Center, restored water-powered gristmill and blacksmith shop in operation, displays of pioneer industries. Open dawn to dusk. The coffee shop serves country lunches, and their specialties are ham and barbecue and old-fashioned home-ground corn and buckwheat cakes. Native highland handicrafts and a large variety of items are sold in the craft shop. In season only, May through October.

For information on parkway visitor facilities, write to: Superintendent, 700 Northwestern Plaza, Asheville, NC 28801 or phone (704) 259-0779 or 259-0760.

Campground fees.

Swannanoa (junction of Skyline Drive and Blue Ridge Parkway; the entrance is above Holiday Inn). A mountaintop Italian Renaissance palace, originally built as an exact replica of a Medici palace in Italy, Swannanoa was the home of Dr. Walter Russell, painter, architect, and sculptor. This fabulous estate, valued in the millions, was built in 1912 by Maj. James Dooley of Richmond as a summer home for his wife. Through the years the house fell into neglect and ruin, and when it was purchased in the late 1940s by Dr. Russell, cows and other animals were wandering freely across the polished marble floors. The Russells completely renovated the palace. Upon her husband's death Mrs. Russell opened the first floor and grounds to the public. Many of Dr. Russell's works of art are displayed, including a sculpture of Mark Twain, who was a close friend.

The tour begins in the palace's great baronial hall with domed ceiling, double marble staircase, and Tiffany stained-glass window, and moves beyond into the gold tapestried ballroom, library, and oak-paneled dining room. The garden, terraced three tiers high with marble walls and steps leading up to a rose-covered marble pergola, contains the figures of the Four Freedoms, which Dr. Russell sculpted for Franklin D. Roosevelt.

Open daily 8 to 6 in summer, 9 to 5 in winter. Admission charge.

Alexandria

Originally settled in 1732 by Scottish merchants, Alexandria was named after John Alexander, a local resident and important landowner. The streets were laid out in 1749 with the assistance of 16-year-old George Washington, who often came here on business and pleasure trips from his Mount Vernon estate. Other famous residents included Gen. Robert E. Lee and George Mason, author of the Virginia Bill of Rights. Henry Clay and Daniel Webster patronized the Apothecary Shop, and the Carlyle House hosted such prominent figures as John Paul Jones, Thomas Jefferson, John Marshall, and Aaron Burr. This historical city has numerous 18th- and 19th-century buildings still standing today which are part of the visitor's self-guided walking tour (see *Ramsay House Visitors Center*).

Carlyle House (121 N. Fairfax St.). John Carlyle, a wealthy Scottish merchant, built this stone mansion in 1752 for his bride. The house contains most of its original rich furnishings, handsome paneling, and elaborate molding. British general Edward Braddock met with five British governors here in 1755 to plan the financing of the French and Indian War. The meeting led to the enactment of the Stamp Act, which eventually provoked the American Revolution. George Washington was commissioned a major in the British Army here under General Braddock.

Open 10 to 5 daily, Sundays 12 to 5. Closed Mondays, Thanksgiving, December 24, Christmas, and New Year's Day. Admission charge.

Cedar Knoll Inn (8 miles south of Alexandria, along the George Washington Parkway). This lovely inn, once part of a farm owned by George Washington, offers dining with a scenic view of the Potomac River, only 1 1/2 miles from Mount Vernon. American cuisine is served in rustic fireside surroundings in winter and on sunny terraces during the summer.

Open daily 11:30 A.M. to 9 P.M., until 11 P.M. (with live entertainment) Friday and Saturday, Sunday brunch 11 to 2. For reservations phone (703) 360-7880.

Christ Church (Cameron and Washington streets). The inside of this lovely Episcopal church remains almost the same as when it was completed in 1773—even most of the window glass is original. Both Robert E. Lee and George Washington, who was a vestryman, worshiped and owned

11

pews here; these are now marked with silver plates. Washington had the church's chandelier brought from England at his own expense. The churchyard contains the graves of many Confederate soldiers. Open 9 to 5 Monday through Saturday, 2 to 5 Sunday, Sunday services 8 A.M. and 10:30 A.M. Closed Thanksgiving, Christmas, New Year's Day, and Memorial Day.

Fort Ward Museum and Park (4301 W. Braddock Rd.). With the start of the Civil War, the North hastily began erecting forts around the capital at Washington to protect it against an attack by land. Alexandria was seized by Union troops, and by late 1862 Fort Ward was the fifth largest fort in a chain of 68 completely encircling the city of Washington. The Northwest Bastion has been restored to its original appearance, even to exact replicas of its old entrance gate and guns mounted and ready to fire. An Officer's Hut and Museum building, both constructed from Mathew Brady Civil War photographs, contain extensive collections of Civil War relics.

Museum open free 9 to 5 Tuesday through Saturday, Sunday 12 to 5. Closed Mondays, Thanksgiving, Christmas, and New Year's Day. Park and picnic area also free, open daily 9 A.M. to sunset.

Gadsby's Tavern Museum (134 N. Royal St.). A stagecoach stop, coffeehouse, hotel, and improvised theatre where traveling troupes of entertainers performed, this tavern was an important center of social life in colonial Virginia. The building is made up of the small City Tavern, built in 1752, and the three-story brick City Hotel, added in 1792.

George Washington recruited militia troops here in 1754 for the campaign against the French and Indians. As president, he attended Birthday Balls held here in his honor.

The interior of the tavern, a fine example of Georgian architecture, has been restored. Exceptional food is also served here, with dining attendants dressed in colonial costume.

Museum open 10 to 5 Tuesday through Saturday, 1 to 5 Sunday. Closed Mondays, holidays. Admission charge.

Grist Mill Historical State Park (on Mount Vernon Highway, VA 235, between Mount Vernon and Woodlawn Plantation). This four-story restored mill is an authentic reproduction of the one operated by George Washington on the Mount Vernon Plantation and stands on the original foundations. It once ground wheat and corn and was the center for a cooper shop, blacksmith shop, and distillery. Replicas of the machinery used in the mill are on display, and exhibits with sound effects show how the mill worked and reproduce the sounds it made.

Open 10 A.M. to 6 P.M. daily Memorial Day to Labor Day. Admission charge. Visitor center.

Gunston Hall Plantation (18 miles south of Alexandria on U.S. 1, then 4 miles east on VA 242). Gunston Hall was the home of George Mason, author of the Virginia Declaration of Rights in 1776, which became the basis for our federal Bill of Rights, the 1789 French Declaration of the Rights of Man, and the Charter of the United Nations. The story-and-a-half home, once the center of a 5,000-acre plantation, contains period furnishings. It took three years to complete the splendid carved woodwork; one notable piece is the pineapple carving in the entrance hall, a popular colonial symbol of hospitality. Dancing classes used to be held here, and records show that the Washington children attended them.

The modern Visitor Center contains a museum of personal items belonging to the Mason family. On the grounds are a restored 18th-century kitchen and schoolhouse. Mammoth boxwood hedges in the formal garden were planted by George Mason to form a maze.

Open daily 9:30 to 5; closed Christmas Day. Admission charge. Picnic area and nature trail. Luncheon and tea served to groups with prior reservations. Write to: Manager, Gunston Hall, Lorton, VA 22079, or phone (703) 550-9220.

Robert E. Lee Boyhood Home (607 Oronoco St.). This historic house was built in 1795 by John Potts, for whom Pottstown, Pennsylvania, is named. Four years later it was bought by William Fitzhugh, whose daughter, Mary, was courted and wed here by George Washington Parke Custis, the adopted son of George Washington. The daughter of this couple was later to marry Robert E. Lee.

The house was sold again in 1812 to Light-Horse Harry Lee, three times governor of Virginia and author of the funeral tribute to Washington, "First in war, first in peace and first in the hearts of his countrymen." Lafayette came here to pay his respects to Mrs. Lee upon the death of her husband in 1824, and a year later young Robert E. Lee left home to enter West Point. This lovely historic home contains most of its original furnishings.

Open 10 to 4 Monday through Saturday, 12 to 4 Sunday, February through December 15. Admission charge.

Lee-Fendall House (429 N. Washington St.). Twenty-one Lees lived here between 1784 and 1903, and both George Washington and Light-Horse Harry Lee, the father of Robert E. Lee, visited frequently. Many rare possessions, including a bed bought from the Mount Vernon Plantation after the death of George Washington, are among the furnishings of the house.

During the Civil War, Union troops would frequently throw a family's belongings out in the yard, set the pile on fire, and then tell the family to save what they could; a desk here from the Bedford Plantation in West Virginia bears the scorch marks of such a fire.

Costumed hostesses give conducted tours, and the gardens are open to visitors. Groups with prior reservations may arrange for "Period tasting" parties, with tea, bisquits, and cakes made from Lee family recipes. Write to: Mrs. Frances Shively, 614 Oronoco St., Alexandria, VA 22314.

Open 10 to 5 Tuesday through Saturday, 12 to 5 Sunday. Closed Mondays and all major holidays. Admission charge.

Mount Vernon (9 miles south of Alexandria on the Mount Vernon Memorial Highway). With all the charm and elegance of its 250 years preserved, this gracious estate attracts more than a million visitors annually. A houseguest once wrote of life here, "They live in great style and with the utmost regularity. Breakfast is at seven o'clock, dinner at three, tea at seven, and supper at nine."

Washington was 16 when he came here to live with his elder half-brother, Lawrence, who originally constructed Mount Vernon in 1743. (Lawrence named the estate in honor of Admiral Edward Vernon, of the British Navy, under whom he served.) George Washington acquired the estate in 1754 after the death of Lawrence by purchasing his sister-in-law's life interest. Five years later Washington brought his bride, Martha, to this expansive riverfront plantation. It was here that he returned in 1797 after serving two terms as president of the United States. Two years later he died.

Mount Vernon as it is seen today was planned by Washington before the Revolution. Between 1754 and 1799 he increased his landholdings from 2,126 acres to more than 8,000 acres, built an extensive group of service buildings or "dependencies," and more than doubled in size the modest nine-room house he had inherited. But try as he might, Washington never succeeded in making Mount Vernon pay; the soil was too poor. Thanks to his wealthy wife, reputedly the richest widow in Virginia when he married her, the Washingtons could afford to import elegant furnishings and to entertain lavishly.

Mount Vernon, home of George Washington

Guided tours are conducted through the authentically furnished main house, where hundreds of Washington's personal possessions are on display, including his sword, clothing, letters, books, and deathbed. About a dozen other buildings—including barn, smokehouse, coach house, tannery, and slave quarters—are open for inspection. A short walk leads to the tombs of George and Martha Washington. Clippings from boxwood hedges planted in 1798 are sold in the Kitchen Garden shop. Due to the popularity of Mount Vernon, early morning visitation is suggested.

Open daily 9 to 5 March through October; 9 to 4 November through February. Admission charge. Restaurant and snack bar; post office. Restaurant open 11 A.M. to 3:30 P.M., 5 P.M. to 10 P.M.; Sunday 11 A.M. to 3:30 P.M. Closed Christmas Eve.

Old Club Restaurant (555 S. Washington St.). George Washington and George Mason were among the builders of this colonial structure, which originally served as a clubhouse overlooking the Potomac River. Guests dine in beamed-ceiling dining rooms, choosing from a menu that includes fine wines, traditional Southern dishes such as Virginia country ham and peanut soup, or seafood fare.

Open 11:30 to 3 and 5 to 9 Tuesday through Thursday, until 10 P.M. Friday; 11:30 to 10 Saturday; and 12 to 9 Sunday. Closed Mondays and Christmas Day. For reservations, phone (703) 549-4555.

Old Presbyterian Meetinghouse (321 S. Fairfax St.). Scottish sea captains and merchants erected this meetinghouse in 1774 as a place of worship for Presbyterians. The clock and exterior walls are original; the interior, badly damaged by fire in 1835, has been carefully restored to its former appearance.

The building in the rear was built in 1787 as a parsonage and now serves as a church office. The graveyard contains the Tomb of the Unknown Soldier of the American Revolution and the grave of the personal physician of George Washington.

Open free daily. Closed Sundays.

Pohick Bay Regional Park (10651 Gunston Rd., in Lorton). This thousand-acre park located near historic Gunston Hall offers swimming in season, boating, camping, picnicking, and miniature golfing.

Open daily. Admission charge to park and activities. For information phone (703) 339-6104.

Pohick Church (16 miles south of Alexandria on U.S. 1; 9301 Richmond Highway). Completed in 1774, this Episcopal church was the parish church of Mount Vernon and Gunston Hall. George Washington surveyed the site, was a member of the building committee, and—with George Mason and George William Fairfax—served as vestryman. The cornice, baptismal font, and walls are original. The restored interior of the church was torn out during the Civil War and used as a stable. The baptismal font had been missing for years until it was found in a farmyard where it was being used as a water trough. The square, high-backed pews, typically colonial, were designed to retain the heat of the charcoal warmers brought by worshipers on chilly, wintry days. Visitors will be interested in the initials and dates cut into the stone around the entrance door; they were left there by visitors in the 1800s.

Guests of the church are seated in Washington's or Mason's pews, if available.

Open weekdays 8 to 4; Sunday services.

The Ramsay House Visitors Center (221 King St.). The town's first mayor, William Ramsay, made his home in this 1724 cottage, the oldest in Alexandria. It now serves as the city's visitor center, with free parking passes, a color film shown daily except Sundays, brochures on a walking tour, maps, and other helpful tour information provided. Phone (703) 838-4200.

Open, free, 10 to 5 daily. Closed Thanksgiving, Christmas, and New Year's Day. Guided walking tours daily April through November.

Stabler-Leadbeater Apothecary Shop (107 S. Fairfax St.). Founded in 1792, this pharmacy was in continuous operation for almost 150 years, and great care has been taken to restore it to its original appearance when it was patronized by such figures as George Washington, Robert E. Lee, Henry Clay, Daniel Webster, and John Calhoun. The shop was also an informal meeting place where residents of Alexandria would gather to listen to impromptu debates between Webster and Calhoun.

The building is original, down to the counters and shelving, and filled with such rare displays as an 1802 note written by Martha Washington asking for a bottle of castor oil; a yellow-leaved pharmacist's book opened to a page showing a formula for "Acidulated Ceyenne Drops," crossed out and marked "Failure"; numerous old bottles; and the largest collection of medicinal glass in the country. A recording gives the history of the shop as visitors browse among the displays.

Free; open 10 to 4:30 Monday through Saturday. Closed Sundays and holidays.

Torpedo Factory Arts Center (105 N. Union St.). Once a munitions plant, the building now houses an artist's center and the city's archaeology offices, labs, and museum.

Open free daily. Closed Thanksgiving, Christmas, and New Year's Day.

George Washington Masonic National Memorial (one mile west on King Street from the center of downtown Alexandria). Towering to a height of 333 feet and modeled after the ancient lighthouse in Alexandria, Egypt, this stunning memorial is devoted to safeguarding the Masonic relics of George Washington, the first Master of the Alexandria-Washington Masonic Lodge. Masons across the country contributed more than $5 million between 1922 and 1932 to finance its construction, on the site first proposed for the nation's Capitol.

A 17-foot bronze statue of George Washington stands in the Great Hall of the first floor, with six other floors displaying the personal effects of Washington and priceless Masonic articles.

The Replica Lodge Room contains Washington's Master's Chair from his library at Mount Vernon, the inscribed silver trowel he used to lay the cornerstone of the nation's Capitol in 1793, and a chamber clock pointing to the moment of his

Masonic Lodge, Alexandria

death, when it was stopped by one of his attending physicians. The Washington family Bible containing family history entries is on exhibit in the George Washington Museum Gallery.

Two elevators take visitors on a 45-minute tour of the seven floors and the Observation Floor, where there is a panoramic view of the surrounding countryside.

Open daily 9 to 5; free. Closed Thanksgiving, Christmas, and New Year's Day.

Woodlawn Plantation and Pope-Leighey House (on U.S. 1, 7 miles south of Alexandria). Lovely Woodlawn plantation, built during the years 1800 to 1805, was a wedding gift from George and Martha Washington to Martha's granddaughter, Eleanor Custis, who married Washington's nephew, Maj. Lawrence Lewis. This elegant residence, designed by William Thornton, first architect of the Capitol building in Washington, D.C., hosted such prominent visitors as Lafayette, Henry Clay, and Andrew Jackson, and still contains many of its rich period furnishings.

19

Visitors will delight in the Touch and Try exhibits in the room adjacent to the Gift Shop. Children can sit at an old student's desk and learn the three Rs with a quill pen and 19th-century textbooks, or play with toys and games that were popular with the Lewis children: hoop-rolling, cup and ball, dancing dolls, block puzzles, and hobbyhorses. Mom can try her hand at needlework on an old sampler, and Dad can practice tying a cravat. In the old days there were elaborate knot variations, and the "Gordian Knot" was so complicated it had to be cut from the neck!

Also located on the spacious wooded grounds is the *Pope-Leighey House,* designed in 1940 by the late Frank Lloyd Wright for suburban life of the mid-20th century. It was moved here when highway construction threatened to demolish it.

Woodlawn is open daily 9:30 A.M. to 4:30 P.M. Closed Thanksgiving, Christmas, and New Year's Day. Admission charge.

Pope-Leighey House open daily 9:30 to 4:30 March through November; Saturdays and Sundays only rest of year. Admission charge.

Amelia

Haw Branch Plantation (12 miles north of Amelia on VA 681, then 3 miles east on VA 667). Col. Thomas Tabb, who started with a single trading post and developed it into a profitable business, built this elegant mansion in 1745. The mansion is of particular interest because it is set in a rectangular, brick-paved depression resembling a dry moat. The estate received its name from the hawthorn-lined stream that fed the plantation millpond, and hawthorn blossoms have been hand-carved in the ornate interior woodwork. A legend (first recorded four generations ago) has it that the rooms are sometimes visited by a ghostly "lady in white," who leaves behind her the scent of roses when she departs.

On the grounds are a kitchen, smokehouse, schoolhouse, weaving room, and hand-hewn log cabin that once housed slaves. Cattle graze on pastures developed in the early 18th century.

Open daily 10 to 5 April through October; rest of year by appointment only, phone (804) 561-2472. Closed Thanksgiving and Christmas Day. Admission charge.

Sayler's Creek Battlefield State Park (9 miles southwest of Amelia on U.S. 360, then 7 miles west on VA 307, 2 miles north on VA 617). The last major battle of the Civil War was fought here on April 6, 1865, just three days before Gen. Robert E. Lee's surrender at Appomattox. There is an auto tour of the park.

Appomattox

Appomattox Court House National Historical Park (3 miles northeast of Appomattox on VA 24). On April 2, 1865, the battle-weary remnant of Lee's Army of Northern Virginia was forced to retreat southwestward from Richmond before the superior forces of General Grant, leaving the Confederate capital completely undefended. Nearly one-third of Lee's forces were killed, wounded, or captured in fierce battles during the retreat, and when the 30,000 remaining Confederate soldiers struggled into the vicinity of Appomattox, they found themselves completely blocked in by the bluecoated infantry.

General Lee, realizing the hopelessness of the situation, reluctantly surrendered. An aide, carrying a white towel as a makeshift flag of truce, was sent to arrange a meeting. On April 9, 1865, the two commanders met in the home of Wilmer McLean, where General Lee accepted and signed the generous terms of the settlement. The few remaining Confederate commands surrendered within weeks, bringing the Civil War at last to an end.

Today the Village of Appomattox Court House has been restored to its 1865 appearance. In the Visitor Center in the reconstructed courthouse there is a 17-minute slide-talk show, free map for the self-guided walking tour, and historical displays, including the towel used as the flag of truce, the pencil Lee used to sign the surrender document, and the table on which it was signed.

In a quiet village setting, there are 11 other restored buildings, most hosted by "living history" characters—people who play parts from history. Some speak in the first person as if they were living in 1865, and others talk as if that were their past; all give different views of the Civil War. The Meeks Country Store is completely supplied as of old, with reproductions of 1860 period items. There is also a county jail, the Woodson Law Office, and the home of the village handyman, all furnished and open for inspection. The imposing, three-story brick McLean House where the surrender occurred has been completely and authentically furnished, right down to the rug in the parlor, an exact copy of the original design.

Sayler's Creek Battlefield State Park, near Amelia, is the site of the last major battle of the Civil War in Virginia.

Open daily 8:30 to 5, September through early June; 8:30 to 6, mid-June to Labor Day. Closed major holidays. Admission charge.

Holliday Lake State Park (9 miles northeast of Appomattox on VA 24, then 6 miles southeast on VA 626, 692). This park has a 150-acre lake, with facilities for fishing and swimming, boat rentals, picnicking, and tent and trailer sites available April through November. A Visitor Center is open daily from 10 to 6 Memorial Day through Labor Day.

Admission charge for activities in the park.

Arlington County

Arlington was made part of the District of Columbia when it was laid out for the capital in 1791, but was returned to Virginia in 1846. Its 25 1/2-square-mile area is mostly residential, with beautiful scenic drives along the Potomac. Among its attractions are the Arlington National Cemetery, the Pentagon, and the National Airport.

For more information, write: Arlington Visitors Service, 2100 N. 14th St., Arlington, VA 22201; or the Arlington Visitors Center, 735 S. 18th St., Alexandria, VA 22202; phone (703) 521-0772 or 521-0773.

Arlington National Cemetery

Located on the Virginia shore of the Potomac River and occupying some 500 acres, this national shrine, established in

1864, contains the graves of over 170,000 servicemen and women, dating from the Revolutionary War to the Vietnam War. Most of the graves are very simply marked, and walking along the shaded paths among all these lives given in the service of their country is a very stirring experience.

The Tomb of the Unknown Soldier (also referred to as the Tomb of the Unknowns) was placed here in 1921. It contains the remains of an unknown American serviceman who died in World War I, and on Memorial Day 1958, two more bodies were added, one unknown soldier from World War II and one unknown from the Korean War. A memorial is inscribed with the following tribute: "Here rests in honored glory an American soldier known but to God." This hallowed place is guarded 24 hours a day. The changing of the guard takes place every hour on the hour.

Two presidents of the United States—William Howard Taft and John Fitzgerald Kennedy—are buried at Arlington National Cemetery. Here, too, are the gravesite of Sen. Robert F. Kennedy, the graves of six American astronauts, and the monuments of the Confederate War Memorial and the Mast of the Battleship *Maine*.

The Memorial Amphitheatre is used for Memorial Day, Easter sunrise, and Veterans Day services as well as other ceremonies.

Arlington House, the Robert E. Lee Memorial, stands on a hill overlooking the Lincoln Memorial. It was built between 1802 and 1817 by George Washington Parke Custis, the adopted son of George Washington and later the father-in-law of Robert E. Lee. Lee married Mary Anna Custis here in 1831, and six of their seven children were born here. George Custis died in 1857, leaving the estate to his daughter.

In 1861, after the outbreak of the Civil War, Lee left Arlington to take command of the Confederate Army of Northern Virginia. The Union army took over the house and grounds as its headquarters for overseeing the defenses of nearby Washington. Forced to flee, Mrs. Lee was notified in 1864 that the federal government had confiscated the estate for nonpayment of property taxes. That same year, a 200-acre section of the 1,100-acre estate was established as a national cemetery. Later, through court action, Robert E. Lee's son regained title to the property. In 1883, he sold it to the United States government for $150,000.

The imposing white mansion, with its massive Doric columns, has been restored to its 1861 appearance. Period furnishings appoint its numerous rooms, which include two dining rooms and two parlors, five bedrooms, an office and study, school and sewing room, kitchen, wine cellar, greenhouse, and 37-foot-long center hall.

At the Arlington National Cemetery Visitor Center, free maps are available and tickets may be purchased for narrated Tourmobile tram rides through the cemetery and to the U.S. Capitol and Washington Mall.

Arlington National Cemetery is open, free, daily 8 A.M. to 7 P.M., April through September; 8 to 5 October through March.

Arlington House is open, free, daily 9:30 to 6 April through September; 9:30 to 4:30 October through March; closed Christmas and New Year's Day.

Iwo Jima Statue, Arlington

Iwo Jima Statue (on Arlington Boulevard). The U.S. Marine Corps Memorial, popularly known as the Iwo Jima Statue, is the largest sculpture ever cast in bronze. Each of the men is over 32 feet high; they are depicted raising the United States flag on Mount Suribachi (on Iwo Jima island in the Pacific) in 1945, from one of the most famous photographs of World War II. Concerts are played on a 49-bell carillon, a gift from the Netherlands, on Saturdays and holidays from 2 to 4 P.M., April through September. Sunset parade late May to late August.

Pentagon Building (bounded by Jefferson Davis Highway, Washington Boulevard, and Shirley Highway). One-hour guided tours are available through this building of more than three million square feet of office space, housing the Department of Defense.

Free; open 9 to 3:30 Monday through Friday. Closed holidays.

Ashland

Kings Dominion (1 mile east of Ashland on VA 54, then 7 miles north on I-95; or 20 miles north of Richmond). Plan to spend all day at this giant $50-million family entertainment complex, where more than 40 rides and 11 shows of live entertainment offer hours of fun. Colorful International Street has German and Italian shops, sidewalk cafes, and a high-speed elevator ride to the top of a replica of the Eiffel Tower. Hanna-Barbera cartoon characters inhabit Happy Land, where there are sporty roadsters to ride over a miniature Grand Prix turnpike course, and a variety of rides for adults and children. Old Virginia features a flume log ride and foot-stomping hoedown at the Virginia Reel Amphitheater. You can test your skill at the games in the Candyapple Grove amusement park, and your nerve on one of the world's fastest double roller coasters. In Lion Country Safari, travel in the air-conditioned comfort of a monorail ride through a jungle of more than 400 wild animals, while lions, white rhinos, elephants, and stately giraffes wander freely in

Kings Dominion, near Richmond

a natural jungle habitat. The Lost World offers four mysterious fantasy rides enclosed in the world's tallest man-made mountain.

Open daily June through Labor Day; weekends only late March through Memorial Day and after Labor Day through early October. Admission charge. For information phone (804) 876-5000.

Scotchtown, Home of Patrick Henry (11 miles northwest of Ashland via VA 54, 671, County 685). Built in the early 1700s, this was the home of Patrick Henry from 1771 to 1778. Patrick Henry was elected the first governor of Virginia under the new nation in 1776; shortly thereafter he took up residence in the Governor's Palace in Williamsburg. Records indicate that at one time Dolley Madison also lived at Scotchtown. The restored manor house is furnished with 18th-century antiques, and the law office, kitchen, and guesthouse have been reconstructed.

Open 10 to 4:30 Monday through Saturday, 1:30 to 4:30 Sundays, April through October. Admission charge.

Basye

Bryce Mountain Resort (11 miles west of Mount Jackson on VA 263 in Basye). In summer, this resort area offers fishing, swimming, boating, horseback riding, tennis, golf, nature trails, and grass-skiing. Winters, snowskiing facilities include chair lifts and rope tows, professional ski instruction, equipment rentals, and ski patrol.

Winters open daily mid-December to mid-March. Cafe and restaurant.

Bryce Mountain Resort Inn. Accommodations include condominiums in a lodge, town houses, and chalets. Entertainment facilities include a swimming pool, playground, 18-hole golf course, lighted indoor tennis court, private beach, bicycle rentals, lawn games, and horseback riding.

For more information, write: Bryce Mountain Resort Inn, Box 3, Basye, VA 22810, or phone (703) 856-2144.

Big Stone Gap

John Fox, Jr., House (Shawnee Avenue). This Virginia Historical Landmark is the beautifully furnished, 1888 home of John Fox, Jr., who wrote *The Trail of the Lonesome Pine*. Made into a movie in 1936, the novel tells the story of feuding families and the changes that come about when the railroad is built on their land. John Fox, Jr., was also the author of *The Little Shepherd of Kingdom Come*, and more than ten full-length novels and 500 short stories.

Open Tuesday through Saturday, June to Labor Day. Admission charge. Guided tours.

June Tolliver Craft House (junction U.S. 23, 58A; Clinton Avenue and Jerome Street). After a guided tour of the John Fox, Jr., House, visitors may wish to see where the heroine of *The Trail of the Lonesome Pine* actually lived. June's parlor and bedroom have been restored and furnished with 19th-century antiques, and there is also a John Fox, Jr., Memorial

Room open for inspection. A craft shop sells locally made mountain crafts.

Open, free, daily 10 to 5 Tuesday through Saturday (until 8:30 P.M. on the nights of the drama), 2 to 6 P.M. Sunday. Closed Christmas week through April.

The Trail of the Lonesome Pine, enjoyable entertainment for the entire family, is performed in an outdoor setting next to the June Tolliver Craft House. Performances 8:30 P.M., Thursday through Saturday, July through August. For reservations write: June Tolliver Playhouse, Big Stone Gap, VA 24219, or phone (703) 523-1235.

Natural Tunnel State Park (18 miles southeast of Big Stone Gap, off U.S. 23). The water action of Stock Creek carved this 850-foot-long, nine-story-high tunnel through a stone ridge over a period of millions of years. Visitors can follow trails through the tunnel, which accommodates a railroad and a river. An adjacent museum (open daily Memorial Day to Labor Day) displays memorabilia of trains that passed through the tunnel in the early 1800s.

Open daily 10 to 6. Admission charge. Swimming, fishing, nature trails. Picnic area and campground atop the tunnel, open April through November.

Southwest Virginia Museum Historical State Park (W. First Street and Wood Avenue). Four floors of area artifacts, relics, and dioramas of pioneer life representing the history of southwestern Virginia are contained in this historical museum. There is an interesting collection of old musical instruments, a set of Minton china presented to British Prime Minister Disraeli by Queen Victoria, farming tools, household gadgets, and souvenirs of the American Revolution and the Civil War.

Open free daily except Mondays, Memorial Day to Labor Day.

Blacksburg

A band of Shawnee Indians massacred a group of white settlers here in 1755 on what is now part of the Virginia

Polytechnic Institute campus. For the story of one of the captives of this Indian raid, see *Radford*.

This area is famous for its spring display of azaleas, rhododendron, and dogwood, and the equally beautiful fall foliage of nearby Jefferson National Forest. The Mountain Lake resort lies 20 miles northwest (on U.S. 460, VA 700). For more information, write: Blacksburg Chamber of Commerce, 141 Jackson St., Blacksburg, VA 24060, or phone (703) 552-4061.

Smithfield Plantation (1/4 mile west of Blacksburg off U.S. 460 Bypass). Col. William Preston built this pre-Revolutionary mansion on land granted to him by King George II. The home stands within the boundaries of the Virginia Polytechnic Institute and State University, although the lands are deeded to the Association for the Preservation of Virginia Antiquities. Colonel Preston's uncle was one of the victims of the 1755 Shawnee Indian massacre. The house has been restored and contains period furnishings and the original woodwork.

Open 1 to 5 Wednesday, Saturday, and Sunday, from April 15 through November 15. Admission charge.

Virginia Polytechnic Institute and State University (on U.S. 460). More than 20,000 students attend what is one of the original Land Grant colleges. There are guided tours through its art and mineral museums.

For more information, contact the Blacksburg Chamber of Commerce (above).

Breaks Interstate Park

(17 miles west of Grundy; 8 miles north of Haysi.) Known as the "Grand Canyon of the South," this five-mile-long and 1,600-foot-deep canyon was carved by the water action of the Russell Fork River. The river winds around the spectacular pyramidal rock formations of the Towers—dating back some 25 million years—which can be viewed from parking overlooks along the paved road skirting the canyon rim.

The 4,800 acres of this park on the Virginia-Kentucky border offer the visitor good bass and bluegill fishing at Laurel Lake, picnicking, paddle boating, pool swimming, riding, camping, and hiking on nature trails. The modern Visitor Center contains exhibits pertaining to the geology and history of the park.

Visitor Center open free daily 9 to 5 April through October. Camping facilities, motor lodge, gift shop, cafe open daily April through October. Cottages all year. Park free; open daily 7 A.M. to 10 P.M. April through October; 7:30 A.M. to 6 P.M. November through March. Park vehicle admission charge Memorial Day through Labor Day. For information, write: Breaks Interstate Park, P.O. Box 100, Breaks, VA 24607, or phone (703) 865-4413 in Haysi, VA.

Bristol

This unique city is situated astride the Virginia-Tennessee state lines, and has two entirely separate city governments. Motorists driving down famous State Street can move from Bristol, Virginia, to Bristol, Tennessee, by simply changing lanes. An ironworks, established here in the 1780s, made the first iron nails for use on the frontier.

For more information on Bristol attractions, write the Greater Bristol Area Chamber of Commerce, 20 Volunteer Parkway, P.O. Box 519, Bristol, VA 24203.

Bristol Caverns (5 miles southeast of Bristol on U.S. 421). This attraction offers unusual stalactite and stalagmite formations, seen on several levels from paved footpaths. An underground river flows through the caverns.

Open 9 A.M. to 8 P.M. Monday through Saturday, from 10 A.M. Sunday, June through Labor Day; open 9 to 6 the rest of the year, from 12 Sunday. Guided tours every 20 minutes; last tour leaves one hour before closing time. Closed Thanksgiving and Christmas Day. Admission charge. Picnic area.

Bristol International Raceway and Thunder Valley Dragway (5 miles south of Bristol on U.S. 11E). Some of the most prestigious racing events in the country are held here. Races in August (phone (615) 764-1161 for information) and drags in May and September (phone (615) 764-3724).

Grand Guitar Museum (off I-81). This unique museum of stringed instruments from all over the world, including more than 200 guitars, is itself in the shape of an acoustic guitar. Open free daily March to December.

Rocky Mount Historic Site (11 miles southwest of Bristol on U.S. 11E). This 18th-century log house, restored to its original appearance, served as the capitol building under William Blount, governor of the Territory of the United States South of the River Ohio. On the grounds are a restored slave cabin, log kitchen, smokehouse, blacksmith shop, and barn.

Open daily. Closed weekends January and February, Thanksgiving, and December 21 through January 5.

South Holston Lake and Dam (8 miles southeast of Bristol on U.S. 421). Bristol is surrounded by five TVA lakes. The nearest is the South Holston Lake, which offers swimming, fishing, boating, and camping facilities. Visitor information may be obtained at the dam's visitor's building, open free daily.

Southern Highland Handicraft Guild Gallery (501 State St.). Locally made mountain handicrafts are sold here.

Open free 10 to 5 Monday through Saturday. Closed Fourth of July, Labor Day, Thanksgiving, and Christmas Day.

Steele Creek Park (3 1/2 miles southwest of Bristol via Broad Street and Volunteer Parkway). More than 900 acres of park and 80 acres of lake offer paddle-boat rentals, golfing, fishing, picnicking, and camping.

Auto admission charge to park; additional admission charge to some of the activities. Picnicking, fishing year round; other activities 9 A.M. to 8 P.M. daily June through mid-September.

Brookneal

Patrick Henry National Memorial (Red Hill Shrine) (3 miles east of Brookneal on VA 600, then 2 miles south on VA

619). Patrick Henry was born at Studley, Hanover County, Virginia, but remotely located Red Hill was where he chose to live after his retirement from public life. This was his last home and burial place.

Patrick Henry (1736–99) became the first governor of Virginia and occupied the governor's palace at Williamsburg for a total of five terms, declining a sixth. As one of the leaders in the movement for America's independence, he inspired patriots to action with such fiery oratory as "United we stand, divided we fall," and "I know not what course others may take, but as for me, give me liberty or give me death!" Credit is also given Patrick Henry for his contribution in leading the movement to adopt the first ten amendments to the Constitution, our national Bill of Rights.

His house and law office have been restored, as have the smokehouse, kitchen, stable, and servants' cabin. A museum and gift shop are also on the grounds. Near the house is his tomb, with the simple inscription, "His fame his best epitaph."

Open 9 to 5 daily, April through October; 9 to 4 November through March. Closed Christmas. Admission charge.

Charles City

The historic James River estates listed below are located between Richmond and Williamsburg on both sides of the James River. During special events, such as the statewide Historic Garden Week, numerous other estates may be opened to the public for brief periods.

Berkeley Plantation (7 miles west of Charles City on VA 5). The Berkeley house was built in 1726 by Benjamin Harrison IV, a leader in colonial affairs. His son, Col. Benjamin Harrison, was a member of the Continental Congress, signer of the Declaration of Independence, and three times governor of Virginia. *His* son was "Old Tippecanoe" William Henry Harrison, a great Indian fighter and the ninth president of the United States, whose inaugural address was written at Berkeley in the room in which he was born. The Harrison family produced yet another president—Benjamin, the grandson of William Henry.

32

The land on which Berkeley stands was part of a grant made in 1619 by King James I to the Berkeley Company. The settlers here held a Thanksgiving Day celebration on December 4, 1619, more than a year before the Pilgrims arrived in New England. President Lincoln came here by boat on two occasions to confer with General McClellan; Master George Thorpe, Episcopal preacher, is credited with making the first bourbon whiskey at the Berkeley Plantation; and Daniel Butterfield, stationed here in 1862, composed the famous tune, the "Taps," now played whenever a man is buried with military honors.

The tour of this plantation literally begins at its gates, where the drive to the house is over a road designed in 1725 for carriages en route to Berkeley. The mansion, looking much as it did 200 years ago, contains historical period furniture. The original furniture and portraits were destroyed in the Revolutionary War by Benedict Arnold, and what was left was burned during the Civil War by General McClellan.

Of special interest in this historic mansion is Benjamin Harrison's signature, discovered during the home's restoration, when removal of the old wallpaper revealed where he

Berkeley Plantation, near Richmond

had written it into the plaster. A frame holds a presidential campaign handkerchief of William Henry Harrison; it shows his birthplace as a log cabin, although he was actually born on the Berkeley Plantation. His study still contains the original door, cut small to his specifications, so the ladies wouldn't be able to get through it in their wide hoop skirts. Embedded in the chimney outside is a cannonball fired in a stray shot during Gen. J. B. Stuart's attack on the Army of the Potomac in 1862. The basement of the house has been made into a museum and contains artifacts found on the grounds of the plantation.

The spacious grounds are open to visitors, and a path leads down to the James River at the site of the first landing by settlers here in 1619.

Open 8 to 5 daily; closed Christmas Day. Admission charge.

The Brandon Plantation, built by Nathaniel Harrison in the 18th century, opens its house to visitors in April during Historic Garden Week, or by appointment; phone (804) 866-8486 or 866-8416. The grounds and gardens, sloping from the house down to the James River, are open daily 9 to 5:30. Admission charge.

Westover was built in the early 1700s by William Byrd, the founder of Richmond. The house is private; the grounds only are open daily 9 to 6. Admission charge.

Both of these estates are located on State Route Virginia 5, between the Berkeley Plantation and Sherwood Forest.

Sherwood Forest, home of John Tyler, Charles City County

Sherwood Forest (4 miles east of Charles City on VA 5). Sherwood Forest, the home of President John Tyler (1841–45), is said to be the longest frame house in America, stretching some 300 feet in length and only one room deep. It was built in the early 1700s and purchased by President Tyler in 1842; he expanded it to its present size. Since that time, the 1,600-acre plantation has been continuously occupied by members of the Tyler family. Visitors are taken on a guided tour through the first-floor rooms, beautifully appointed with 18th- and 19th-century family heirlooms.

Many of the oriental pieces were gifts from the Emperor of China to President Tyler in gratitude for opening the trade routes to China. The dining room contains a rare tea service which originally belonged to Meriwether Lewis of the Lewis and Clark expedition, and a silver urn that belonged to Capt. Alfred Hart Miles, Tyler's grandson-in-law and composer of the famous tune "Anchors Aweigh." Inflation-conscious visitors will find the small, 1830s table in the drawing room of special interest. Called a tea poy, it has four separate compartments for holding the different types of tea, containers for mixing the tea to suit each taste, and a sturdy lock on the front. The lock was not superfluous, because at this time in Virginia tea was selling for $80 per pound!

Sherwood Forest was under Union occupation during the Civil War, and the hall floor and table still bear scorch marks from Union General Butler's attempts to burn the house. Only heroic action by a maid, who carried burning hay out of the house in her bare arms, saved the home. Julia Tyler, the widow of the president (who died in 1862), had fled from the plantation with her five younger children when word was received that General Butler was approaching. She singlehandedly sailed down the James River, out into the Atlantic, through the Union Blockade, and straight to Bermuda. She sold the five bales of cotton she had taken with her for $15,000, remaining in Bermuda for six months to nurse her youngest child through the yellow fever. She sailed back again through the blockade to Gardiner's Island, returning in 1867 to Sherwood Forest, where she remained until her death.

Grounds open daily 9 to 5. House by appointment only,

minimum of four people; closed Christmas. Phone (804) 829-5377. Admission charge.

Shirley Plantation (9 miles west of Charles City on VA 5). Shirley Plantation was founded in 1613 and the present mansion was begun in 1723. Today the 800-acre James River estate is owned and operated by the ninth generation descended from the original owners. Anne Hill Carter was born here, and her son, Robert E. Lee, spent part of his childhood at this plantation.

The tour covers the first floor of the house, which contains family portraits, a collection of crested English silver, and original period furniture. The home is especially famous for its carved walnut staircase, rising three floors without visible support.

On the plantation grounds are the original 1723 brick outbuildings, including a large, two-story kitchen, laundry house, and two barns, one with an ice cellar beneath it. Other original structures include the stable, smokehouse, and dovecote.

Open daily 9 to 5; last tour at 4:30. Closed Christmas Day. Admission charge.

Charlottesville

Situated among the foothills of the beautiful Blue Ridge Mountains, this city was the home of such prominent figures as President James Monroe, Thomas Jefferson, and Meriwether Lewis and William Clark, the explorers of the Louisiana Territory. Many of the mansions on the old estates in this area, some open to the public in April during Virginia's annual Historic Garden Week, were designed by Thomas Jefferson.

The Thomas Jefferson Visitors Center (off the Monticello exit of I-64) offers a historical exhibit entitled "Thomas Jefferson at Monticello." The Center also provides maps, brochures, and free local reservation services. Write Thomas Jefferson Visitors Center, P.O. Box 161, Charlottesville, VA 22902 or phone (804) 293-6789 or 977-1783.

Ash Lawn (2 1/2 miles beyond Monticello; 5 miles southeast of Charlottesville, on County 795). James Monroe's simple residence, popularly known as Ash Lawn, from the great ash trees on the grounds, was built in 1799. The home was designed and built on the house site selected by Monroe's friend and neighbor, Thomas Jefferson. Monroe held more major offices than any other president: U.S. senator; minister to England, to Spain, and to France, where he negotiated the Louisiana Purchase; governor of Virginia; secretary of state and war; author of the Monroe Doctrine; and fifth president of the United States in 1817.

William and Mary College, the alma mater of both Monroe and Jefferson, owns the estate and maintains the residence and gardens. The century-old boxwood garden has a vista facing Monticello, and it is known that Monroe and Jefferson used some sort of coded signal to communicate with each other across the distance. They also visited one another frequently to discuss politics and affairs of state. A statue of Monroe—created by the noted sculptor Piccirilli—stands in the garden, and several outbuildings have been restored. The small house contains many of its original, modest furnishings, which reflect the fact that Monroe was a farmer's son and never acquired much wealth in his lifelong career as a public servant. Finances forced its sale in 1826.

Special events on this 550-acre estate include operas, plays, concerts, and a colonial crafts weekend. Spinning and weaving demonstrations, boxwood gardens with peacocks. Picnic area.

Open daily 9 to 6 March through October; 10 to 5 November through February. Closed Thanksgiving, Christmas, and New Year's Day. Admission charge.

Michie Tavern and Museum (2 1/2 miles southeast of Charlottesville, on VA 53). Built in 1735, this was Patrick Henry's boyhood home until 1746, when it was sold to John Michie. In 1784 it was moved to another location and turned into a tavern, the hotels of colonial days. Letters and guest logs show that President James Monroe entertained General Lafayette as his guest at dinner at Michie's Tavern. General Jackson stopped at the tavern on his way to Washington from his New Orleans campaign, and Jefferson, Madison, and

Monroe met here on one occasion. The very first evening of waltzing to take place in this country is recorded as having shocked the guests in the tavern's ballroom. Michie's descendants owned the tavern until 1910. In 1927 the tavern was dismantled piece by piece and moved to this present site where it was painstakingly reconstructed. The tavern contains one of the largest and finest collections of pre-Revolutionary furniture and artifacts, including many of the original tavern furnishings. Outside are a restored smokehouse, springhouse, and gristmill. An entire 18th-century village is presently under construction.

Visitors to Monticello and Ash Lawn, both along the same road as the tavern, may wish to dine on food of yesteryear served in "The Ordinary," adjacent to the tavern. This building was used 200 years ago as a slave cabin and still has the original logs cut and shaped by hand. The bill of fare features typical dishes of the colonial period—light wines, fried chicken, black-eyed peas, coleslaw, stewed tomatoes, homemade biscuits, corn bread, and apple cobbler. Lunch only is served, from 11:30 A.M. to 3 P.M.

Open 9 to 5 daily. Closed Christmas and New Year's Day. Admission charge.

Meadow Run Grist Mill at Michie Tavern has been in operation for almost 160 years, its two-story-high waterwheel and gears still being turned by a millrace. The adjacent General Store is authentically outfitted, with goods available for purchase. Also housed here is *Virginia's Wine Museum.* The wine industry in Virginia from Jamestown in 1607 to the present is featured, with Virginia wines available for purchase.

Monticello (2 miles southeast of Charlottesville, on VA 53). Thomas Jefferson, author of the Declaration of Independence, founder of the University of Virginia, governor of Virginia, vice-president, and third president of the United States, made his home at Monticello on a 1,000-acre estate inherited from his father in 1757. Located atop the level plateau of a mountain, the estate was named "Monticello," Italian for "Little Mountain," by Jefferson.

Jefferson was an inventive architect and scientist as well as

Monticello, designed and built by Thomas Jefferson

statesman. The 35-room structure, which he designed and built over a 41-year period beginning in 1768, has unique architectural details and devices he originated. In the entrance hall stands a seven-day clock, which also tells the day of the week as cannonball weights descend beside day markers on the wall. Access to the two upper floors is by means of narrow, winding stairways to doors that could be closed off to make the house easier to heat in winter. The parlor doors open simultaneously when one is set ajar, the kitchen pantry door revolves to provide more shelf space and easier access, and a weather vane tells wind direction whether the observer is indoors or outside.

The most prominent feature of the house is the dome, which commands the west or garden front, and it is this view of Monticello which appears on our U.S. nickel. Set in the hillsides under terraces are a kitchen, dairy, smokehouse, laundry, icehouse, servant's quarters, carriage house, and stables; on other plantations, these were in separate outbuildings or "dependencies." The garden and walks remain as Jefferson himself laid them out, even to the plants in each bed, carefully recorded in his garden and farm books. The garden and outbuildings, all furnished, are open for inspection, including Jefferson's "bachelor's quarters." This was the first outbuilding completed on the estate, and Jefferson moved in here when his father's house burned in 1771. This was also where he brought his bride, Martha Wayles Skelton, one year later.

The guided tour covers the first floor of the house, furnished with such rare historical pieces as the bed in which Jefferson died at the age of 83, on July 4, 1826, the exact day of the 50th anniversary of the Declaration of Independence. The family graveyard where he lies buried is nearby.

Open daily 8 to 5 March through October; 9 to 4:30 November through February. Closed Christmas Day. Admission charge. Picnic area.

University of Virginia (west end of Main Street). Thomas Jefferson founded this university and designed many of its buildings. The one-brick-thick serpentine fences, also of Jefferson's design, are famous for their economy, strength, and beauty. Historical tours include the room once occupied by an illustrious former student, Edgar Allan Poe. Woodrow Wilson was also a student here.

Free tours leaving from the Rotunda. Closed three weeks in December. Phone (804) 924-1019.

Chincoteague-Assateague

Connected to the mainland by highway (VA 175, from U.S. 13), Chincoteague Island is a major fishing port and a popular sport fishing area. A bridge from the town leads to Assateague, an island 37 miles long, where there are wildlife tours of the Chincoteague National Wildlife Refuge. This lovely natural habitat is the home of the famous wild ponies that are rounded up to make their annual swim from Assateague across the channel to Chincoteague, where they are auctioned off to visitors.

Chincoteague Island boasts wide, sandy beaches, cottage rentals, camping facilities, motel accommodations, boat rentals, and fine dining. For a relaxing change of pace, try the bed-and-breakfast Channel Bass Inn. Phone (804) 336-6148. The National Park Service provides lifeguarded beaches, bathhouse facilities, snack bar, conducted walks, and evening programs. One of the popular visitor attractions is the Chincoteague Miniature Pony Farm (on Deep Hole

Road). For seafood dining with a waterfront view, try the Landmark Crab House (North Main Street), where even the salad bar is an old crab float. For visitor information, write: Chincoteague Chamber of Commerce, P.O. Box 258, Chincoteague Island, VA 23336, or phone (804) 336-6161.

N.A.S.A. Wallops Flight Center (Route 175, off Route 13). Visitors can see a missile range control center, watch huge radar dishes tracking satellite launches, visit a helicopter hangar, and take a trip through the restricted Wallops Island launch area. The tour begins at the Main Gate Parking Area, where there is a display of some of the typical rockets launched from Wallops. Here visitors are taken aboard air-conditioned buses for a two-hour guided tour, which includes a 15-minute color movie on N.A.S.A.'s current aeronautics and space research. If a launch occurs during the tour, visitors will be permitted to watch from a safe distance.

Open free by reservation only, 10 A.M. and 2 P.M., Monday through Friday, June through August. No tours on weekends, holidays, and days when major launches are scheduled. Reservations suggested a week in advance. Contact the Public Affairs Office, phone (804) 824-1000, 8 to 4:30 Monday through Friday.

Oyster Museum (Assateague Beach Road). This museum features collections of shells and fossils, implements of the fishing industry, a photo history of the settlement of Chincoteague and Assateague, and live marine exhibits.

Open daily, May to September 10; Saturdays and Sundays September 11 to November. Closed December through April. Admission charge.

Refuge Waterfowl Museum (Maddox Boulevard). Antique bird decoys, including two of the rarest decoys known, are on display here. This nautical museum also features boats, weapons, traps, art, and carvings, combined with various outdoor exhibits.

Open daily Memorial Day to Labor Day; Saturdays and Sundays rest of year. Closed Christmas. Admission charge.

Wildlife Tours. Narrated tours of the Chincoteague National Wildlife Refuge on Assateague Island are on Cruise

Ship *Osprey* or by enclosed trams that travel through the center of the refuge, not ordinarily accessible by car. Ocean fishing excursions available June through August; charter only September through May.

Cruise ships leave daily June through August. Wildlife Tram Safari leaves daily June through August, weekends only September through November. For a schedule and fees, write: Island Cruises, Inc., P.O. Box 173, Chincoteague Island, VA 23336, or phone (804) 336-5593 or 336-5511.

Further information is available at Tom's Cove Visitor Center (open daily) and at the Chincoteague Refuge Visitors Center (open daily spring to fall). Or write Refuge Manager, Chincoteague National Wildlife Refuge, P.O. Box 62, Chincoteague, VA 23336; or phone (804) 336-6122.

Clarksville

Occoneechee State Park (1 1/2 miles east of Clarksville on U.S. 58). A picturesque lake and more than 2,000 acres of park provide boating, fishing, swimming, camping, picnicking, water-skiing, and concession facilities.

Open daily April through November. Admission charge to facilities. For information phone (804) 374-2210.

Prestwould Plantation (2 miles north of Clarksville on U.S. 15). Sir Peyton Skipwith, American-born baronet, built this stone manorial plantation home in 1795. The house sits on a high knoll overlooking Roanoke River and is shaded by a giant oak, 27 feet in circumference and more than 300 years old. Original furnishings and scenic wallpapers grace the interior. The house and fences were constructed of stone quarried on the plantation. Several of the original outbuildings are preserved and some have been restored.

Open daily May through September; weekends only in October. Admission charge.

Clifton Forge

Douthat State Park (5 miles north of Clifton Forge on VA 629). Swimming, fishing, and boating (rentals available) on a

70-acre lake, picnicking, camping, and small lodge and cabin facilities are available in this park of more than 4,000 acres. A visitor center offers evening programs.

Camping April through November. Phone (703) 862-7200.

Iron Gate Gorge (2 miles south of Clifton Forge on U.S. 220). Towering walls of rock rise above the banks of the Jackson River. A forge that operated for nearly a century has been restored.

Covington

Fort Young (near exit 4 on I-64). This fort, a reconstruction, was built from architectural plans drawn by George Washington. The original fort was located near this site.

Humpback Bridge (3 miles west of Covington off U.S. 60, I-64). Built in 1835 and in use until 1929, this bridge was made of hand-hewn timber and joined with wooden pegs and handmade bolts. It is the only covered bridge of this type of construction now standing in the United States.

Culpeper

In 1749 Culpeper was surveyed by 17-year-old George Washington, who received his surveyor's licence here. The residence where he stayed still stands on Spencer Street. Culpeper Minute Men were organized in 1775, and two years later marched with volunteers from Fauquier and Orange counties to Williamsburg in answer to Patrick Henry's call to arms. Their flag pictured a coiled rattlesnake, with the inscriptions "Don't tread on me" and "Liberty or Death." During the Civil War many of the town's buildings were turned into hospitals for wounded soldiers.

Culpeper Cavalry Museum (133 W. Davis St.). This museum contains Civil War weapons, cavalry equipment, and other historical artifacts.

Open Monday through Friday. Closed Christmas, New Year's Day, and Fourth of July.

Danville

The first woman to sit in the British House of Commons, Nancy Langhorne, Viscountess Astor, was born in Danville in 1879.

Tobacco auctions, open to the public, are held here from mid-August through early November, 9 to 2:30 Monday through Thursday; closed Labor Day, Columbus Day, and Veterans Day. Danville's auction market, one of the nation's largest, is a colorful sales process dating back to the late 1800s. The largest single-unit textile mill in the world, Dan River, Inc., is also located here.

Every September during Danville's Harvest Jubilee, the city hosts the World Tobacco Auctioneering Championship to determine who is the world's best tobacco auctioneer.

For more information contact the Chamber of Commerce, 635 Main St., P.O. Box 1538, Danville, VA 24543; or phone (804) 793-5422.

Chatham (17 miles north of Danville on U.S. 29). A self-guided walking tour around this town includes an Educational and Cultural Center with museum, planetarium, antique shops, and restaurants; the Hargrave Military Academy; 1894 Chatham Hall; 1813 Old Clerk's Office; 1860s Sims-Mitchell House; 1853 Courthouse; and 1844 Emmanuel Episcopal Church.

For information write the Chamber of Commerce, 38 Main St., Chatham, VA 24531; or phone (804) 432-1650.

National Tobacco-Textile Museum (614 Lynn St.). The museum's Tobacco Room contains thousands of collections gathered from all over the world: cigarette packs, pipes, lighters, ashtrays, and posters. The Textile Room recounts the history of this industry, with a model of a textile mill, samples of cloth dating back to the 19th century, and old looms, spinning wheels, and sewing machines. A small library documents the history of both industries.

Open 10 to 4 Tuesday through Friday, 2 to 4 Saturday and Sunday. Closed major holidays. Admission charge.

The Sutherlin House, "Last Capitol of the Confederacy" (975 Main St.). On April 3, 1865, President Jefferson Davis, his cabinet, and the administrative officers of the Confederacy, having fled Richmond upon Lee's retreat toward Lynchburg, were received by Major Sutherlin in his home in Danville. For a week the "Confederate government" made the Sutherlin House its last "Capitol," until news of Lee's surrender at Appomattox forced them to flee south.

Parts of the house have been restored to their original appearance, with many family portraits, personal belongings, and original furnishings on display. The residence also houses the Danville Museum of Fine Arts, with exhibits (on loan from museums nationwide) changed monthly.

Free; open 10 to 5 Tuesday through Friday, 2 to 5 Sunday. Closed major holidays.

Dismal Swamp National Wildlife Refuge

The Dismal Swamp, though greatly reduced by drainage from its original 2,000-square-mile area to less than 600 square miles, is still a large, tree-covered swampland. It is a vast landscape of peat bogs, thickets of vines and brier, twisted cypress stumps, and valuable hardwood trees. The dense forests and tangled undergrowth attract sportsmen and naturalists, but lumbering is carried on only with great difficulty. Animal life abounds here—black bear, wildcats, foxes, and a great many poisonous reptiles.

In 1728 this area was visited by William Byrd, who suggested the need for an inland waterway from the mouth of the Chesapeake Bay area to Albemarle Sound, North Carolina. George Washington organized a company called Adventurers for Draining the Great Dismal Swamp, which drained most of the swamp and cut through a canal, completed in 1805. It was used to transport products—mostly cedar shingles—between Norfolk and the sounds of North Carolina. The canal leads to a lake near the center of the swamp, Lake Drummond, once valued by ships for its drinking water because it kept its freshness for long periods of time. Harriet Beecher Stowe used the swamp as the scene of her 1856 antislavery novel, *Dred*.

Boat tours, fishing, camping, bird-watching, and photography are some of the activities popular in the area. For further information, write: Superintendent, 358 George Washington Highway, Dismal Swamp, VA 23323; or phone (804) 485-1114.

Eastville

The county seat of Northampton, Eastville's 1730 courthouse, is the oldest standing courthouse building in the United States. It contains the oldest continuous court records in the nation, dating from 1632, including the only record of a local court's declaration that the English Parliament's Stamp Act was unconstitutional. On Court House Square are a 1719 Clerk's Office and a 1644 Debtor's Prison.

Fairfax

For information on county parks, write: Fairfax County Park Authority, 3701 Pender Dr., Fairfax, VA 22030; or phone (703) 246-5700.

Fairfax Court House (4000 Chain Bridge Rd.). Built in 1799, this courthouse contains the wills of George and Martha Washington, on display for visitors. A monument to Capt. John Q. Marr, the first Confederate soldier killed in the Civil War, stands on the grounds.

Open, free, daily 8 A.M. to 4 P.M.; closed holidays.

George Mason University (4400 University Dr.). The largest collection of material relating to the Federal Theatre Project of the 1930s is kept in the Fenwick Library here. There are stage sets, costume designs, and scripts, including some unpublished works by Arthur Miller.

Open 8 A.M. to 11 P.M. Monday through Thursday, until 5 P.M. Fridays. Closed major holidays.

Sully Plantation (10 miles west of Fairfax on U.S. 50, then north on VA 28). This was the home of Richard Bland Lee, the brother of Gen. Light-Horse Harry Lee. The house was built in 1794 and remains virtually unchanged today, with only minor repairs. It contains some of the original furnishings, and on the grounds are a kitchen-washhouse and smokehouse.

Open daily 10 to 5, 12 to 5 Sundays, March through December. Closed Tuesdays, Thanksgiving, Christmas, and New Year's Day. Admission charge. Picnic area.

Wolf Trap Farm for the Performing Arts (in Vienna, 8 miles northeast of Fairfax on VA 123, then west on U.S. 7 to Trap Road—follow signs). Renowned artists of dance, jazz, opera, folk music, and musical theatre perform on stage, where the Filene Center open theatre seats 3,700 people, with room for 3,000 more on the sloping lawn for those who wish to take picnics and enjoy the programs under the stars. On nonperformance days, the 117 acres of the park are open to those who wish to hike, bicycle, or picnic. Activities include live theatre performances summers for children, an annual International Children's Festival in mid-September, art workshops, and afternoon band concerts.

Performances early June through early September. For a schedule and mail-order form, write: Wolf Trap Box Office, 1624 Trap Road, Vienna, VA 22180, or phone (703) 255-1860. Tickets can also be reserved at Ticketron, Inc. outlets throughout the eastern U.S. The Wolf Trap Box Office is open daily 12 to 6 P.M. on nonperformance days, 12 to 9 P.M. on performance days. Snack bar and refreshments.

Barns of Wolf Trap Foundation (3/4 mile south of Wolf Trap Farm on Trap Road). A combination conference center and 350-seat theatre, with chamber music, jazz, and other performing arts.

Open seasonally. For information, write the Barns, 1635 Trap Rd., Vienna, VA 22180, or phone (703) 938-2404.

Falls Church

Falls Episcopal Church (115 E. Fairfax St. at Washington Street, on U.S. 29, 211). The original Falls Church was built in 1734 and named for the Little Falls of the Potomac River. The present structure was built on the original site in 1767–69. It served as a recruiting station during the American

Revolution. During the Civil War it was used as a hospital, and later as a stable. The church has been restored to its original appearance.

Open daily 9 to 4. Closed Christmas and New Year's Day.

Fredericksburg

From 1739 to 1747, George Washington lived on a small farm just outside Fredericksburg. This is where the legend of the cherry tree originated, where he learned surveying, and where his father died. Fredericksburg was called by Washington "the place of my growing infancy," and he visited the city frequently throughout his life. His sister lived here in a beautiful Georgian mansion, and close by was the last home of Washington's mother.

James Monroe had his law office here, and the offices, homes, and shops were frequented by Thomas Jefferson, generals Hugh Mercer and George Weedon, Adm. John Paul Jones, Patrick Henry, and other famous Americans.

Four of the major battles of the Civil War were fought in this area, with the city of Fredericksburg changing hands no less than seven times between Confederate and Union forces. The battlefields are preserved in the nearby Fredericksburg and Spotsylvania National Military Park, and the 40-block National Historic District of Fredericksburg contains one of the largest collections of 18th- and 19th-century buildings in the United States.

At the Visitor Center, 706 Caroline St., phone (703) 373-1776, there are free maps, a film, parking passes for metered zones, and ticket information to the stops on the Historic Tour.

Belmont (off I-95, Route 17 east, at 224 Washington St. in Falmouth). The American artist Gari Melchers (1860–1932) lived in this gracious 18th-century house, now a memorial art gallery. Melchers received many awards and decorations, both here and abroad, and his pictures are owned by galleries throughout the western world. The awards and a large sampling of his works—as well as other antiques, artworks, and rare furnishings, many collected by Melchers and his wife during their residences in Europe—are exhibited in his Belmont home and stone studio. The grounds offer visitors a pleasant stroll along a boxwood promenade, with a splendid view of the wooded Rappahannock River Valley.

Open Mondays, Wednesdays, Fridays, Saturdays, and Sundays from 1 to 4 P.M. Closed Tuesdays, Thursdays, Christmas, and New Year's Day. Admission charge.

Fredericksburg Masonic Lodge (Princess Anne and Hanover streets). George Washington was initiated a Mason into this lodge on November 4, 1752, although the present building dates only from 1812. Relics from his initiation are on display, and include the Bible used in his obligation, the Minute Book recording the event, and the Master's Canopy, ridden with bullet holes when it was damaged during the heavy fighting in the city during the Civil War.

Open 9 to 12 and 1 to 4 Monday through Saturday, 1 to 4 Sunday. Closed Thanksgiving, Christmas, and New Year's Day. Admission charge.

Kenmore (1201 Washington Ave.). Col. Fielding Lewis, a prominent citizen in 18th-century Virginia, built Kenmore between the years 1752 and 1756 on an 863-acre plantation overlooking the Rappahannock River. The house was built

Kenmore, home of Betty Washington, Fredericksburg

for Lewis's second wife, Betty, the only sister of George Washington.

The large and modern Information Center contains an impressive diorama of Fredericksburg in 1765 and a recording of the history of Kenmore, plus artifacts belonging to the Washington and Lewis families.

The guided tour of the house takes visitors through rooms lavish with carved moldings and architectural details reflecting Lewis's efforts to retain his English identity. Rare historical furnishings include a game table that once belonged to the Washington family, a tea service belonging to Alexander Hamilton, and a desk chair belonging to Patrick Henry, all visitors at Kenmore. Most of the furnishings are 18th-century antiques not original to the house, the family furnishings and lands having been sold to pay Colonel Lewis's debts. He died penniless in 1782, having spent his entire savings on manufacturing weapons for the Revolutionary troops led by his brother-in-law, George Washington.

The house has a cannonball still embedded in the outside back wall, with bullet holes in the porch columns, a reminder that the Civil War touched here. A walk through the lovely restored gardens takes the visitor to the plantation's kitchen. Many rare colonial kitchen utensils and tools are on display and free tea and gingerbread, made from Betty Lewis's original recipe, are served.

Open daily 9 to 5, March through November; 10 to 4 during the rest of the year. Closed Thanksgiving, December 24, 25, and 31, and January 1. Admission charge. Gift shop.

Hugh Mercer Apothecary Shop (1020 Caroline St.). One of the oldest apothecary shops in the United States, this shop, established in 1771, remains just as it was in the 18th century, with original glass bottles, silver- and gold-plated medicine pills, huge hand-blown jars intricately painted from the inside, faded prescriptions, ornate showcases, and the doctor's original desk for prescription writing.

As was the custom of those days, Dr. Mercer combined the practices of medicine and pharmacy and had a medical office and surgery adjoining the shop. A sitting room connecting with a small library was used by George Washington, a close friend of Mercer's, during his business trips to Fredericksburg. Washington's expense accounts are open to view here. Upstairs are the living quarters and a small wig room; as was the custom, gentlemen would stick their wigged heads through a hole in the door while a servant seated inside applied white powder to keep the wigs looking clean and fresh.

With the outbreak of the American Revolution, Dr. Mercer was appointed brigadier general in the Continental Forces and served under his friend, George Washington. On January 2, 1777, Mercer received a mortal wound in a British bayonet charge; he died three weeks later.

Open daily 9 to 5, April through October; seasonal hours November through March. Closed December 24, 25, and 31, and January 1. Admission charge.

James Monroe Law Office and Museum (908 Charles St.). After studying law with Thomas Jefferson, James Monroe began his practice in this brick building in 1786, launching a career of public service that would lead him to more high offices than have been held by any other U.S. president. He was negotiator of the Louisiana Purchase, four times governor of Virginia, secretary of state, secretary of war, twice

James Monroe Law Office and Museum, Fredericksburg

president of the United States, and author of the Monroe Doctrine.

Among the many exhibits in the museum are the Louis XVI desk, with hidden compartments, on which the Monroe Doctrine was signed, and President and Mrs. Monroe's elegant velvet court costumes, worn when they were presented at the court of Napoleon. The Monroes' Louis XVI furniture on display here was used by them in the White House. In 1932, Mrs. Herbert Hoover, wife of the president of the United States, had copies of this furniture made, which are in the White House today. The Memorial Library adjoining the museum contains rare books, historic documents, and State and family correspondence.

The small garden contains a mulberry tree, growing when Monroe was practicing law, and a bronze bust of Monroe by Cresson.

Open daily 9 to 5; closed Thanksgiving, December 24, 25, and 31, and January 1. Admission charge.

Rising Sun Tavern (1306 Caroline St.). Built in 1760 by Charles, the youngest brother of George Washington, the Rising Sun Tavern served as an important social and political meeting place in 18th-century Fredericksburg. Such notables as George Washington, Patrick Henry, John Marshall, Thomas Jefferson, and other colonial patriots gathered here to discuss the important issues of the day. It was the town's post office, the stagecoach stop, and an important center for news from the other colonies. Balls were held here, traveling entertainers performed, and gentlemen met to amuse themselves at the gaming tables and bowling on the green.

The restored frame building has never been structurally altered, and it is authentically furnished with late 18th-century English and American pieces. Among the interesting items are a desk owned by Thomas Jefferson, blue glass fingerbowls used by Jefferson and Lafayette, and chairs belonging to James Monroe. The bar has been restored in the Tap Room, which is furnished with gaming tables, checkers carved from a whale's backbone, boot racks, tavern pewter, and other authentic accessories. In the gentlemen's chambers, as many as four men often had to share the same small bed. Gentlemen were thoughtfully required by law to remove their boots before retiring.

Tours conducted by costumed hostesses. Spiced tea served to visitors.

Open daily 9 to 5, April through October; seasonal hours November through March. Closed Thanksgiving, December 24, 25, and 31, and January 1. Admission charge.

Shannon Air Museum (2 miles south of Fredericksburg on VA 2 and U.S. 17 at Shannon Airport). This museum was dedicated to Sidney L. Shannon, aviation pioneer who, along with Eddie Rickenbacker, worked in the development of Eastern Airlines. In addition to the antique aircraft on display, there are displays of engines and aeronautical gear, a small replica of an early aeronautical machine shop, a theatre where aviation movies and slides are shown, and an aviation library.

Open daily 9 to 5. Closed Thanksgiving, Christmas, and New Year's Day. Admission charge. Restaurant at Shannon Airport.

Mary Washington Grave (Washington Avenue at end of Pitt Street). A large granite shaft, dedicated in 1894 by President Grover Cleveland, is the resting place of Mary Ball Washington, mother of George Washington. Behind the monument is Meditation Rock, where she often went for walks with her grandchildren.

Mary Washington House (1200 Charles St.). George Washington bought this lovely Dutch Colonial cottage for his mother, who lived here from 1772 until her death in 1789. Many of Mrs. Washington's personal belongings are here, including her childhood Book of Meditation, the Chippendale mirror she willed to George Washington and his wife, and a secretary. The beautiful hand-carved woodwork of the mantels and paneling is original. One unusual 18th-century period piece is a wooden cheese dish on wheels that could be rolled up and down the dining table.

The charming English garden behind the house still has Mrs. Washington's sundial and some of the boxwood she planted.

Open daily 9 to 5, April through October; seasonal hours November through March. Closed December 24, 25, and 31, and January 1. Admission charge.

Fredericksburg and Spotsylvania National Military Park

Parts of four battlefields are contained in this park, where Union and Confederate armies fought the battles of Fredericksburg, Chancellorsville, the Wilderness, and Spotsylvania Court House. The Confederates won the first two, but Federal successes in the last two engagements ultimately led to the destruction of the Confederate Army of Northern Virginia.

Fredericksburg, directly in the path of Federal invasion from Washington to Richmond and the capital of the Confederacy, was attacked on December 13, 1862, by more than 142,000 Union troops under the command of General Burnside. Confederate forces under General Lee numbered only 92,000 men, but after sustaining repeated attacks they succeeded in driving the Federal troops back across the Rappahannock River.

After this disastrous defeat, with Federal losses of over 12,000 compared to Confederate losses of only about 5,000, President Lincoln replaced Burnside with Joseph Hooker. Hooker reorganized the demoralized Federal army and launched another attack against Lee's forces on April 27, 1863, from a site ten miles from Fredericksburg at Chancellorsville. Federal forces numbered more than 133,000 men, over twice the Confederate strength, but once again they were forced to retreat with heavy losses. The Confederates had won their second great victory, but they suffered the tragic loss of Gen. "Stonewall" Jackson, mistakenly shot by his own men.

Gen. Ulysses S. Grant was now placed in charge of all Union armies, although he made his headquarters with the Army of the Potomac. In early May 1864, Federal forces were ordered to move between Lee and Richmond in another attempt to capture the Confederate capital. Lee countered by attacking the Federals in a dense forest west of Fredericksburg known as the Wilderness. Fighting here ended in a stalemate, but broke out again when swift drives to the south brought both forces together at Spotsylvania Court House on May 8, 1864. After 13 days of heavy fighting, Grant again sidestepped Lee's forces and continued his relentless move south towards Richmond. After repeated clashes, Grant eventually reached Petersburg, where both forces dug in for a long and bloody siege that lasted ten months. In April 1865, Petersburg and Richmond fell. A week later, Lee surrendered.

The Fredericksburg Visitor Center and Museum are located on U.S. 1, Lafayette Boulevard. The Fredericksburg National Cemetery contains the graves of more than 15,000 Federal soldiers, miles of trenches, and gun pits.

The Chancellorsville Visitor Center is located at the Chancellorsville Battlefield, ten miles west of Fredericksburg on Route 3. Park Rangers are on hand to give information at both centers, with free maps available for the self-guided tours. Living History programs are held during the summer months.

Free, open 9 to 5 daily with extended summer hours. Closed Christmas and New Year's Day. Picnic area.

Chatham Manor. This wealthy tobacco planter's house was taken over and used as the Federal command headquarters during two of the battles of Fredericksburg. It was also converted to a hospital, where Walt Whitman and Clara Barton (who organized the American National Red Cross in 1881) cared for the wounded.

Open, free, daily 9 to 5; closed Christmas and New Year's Day.

The Old Salem Church (1 mile west of I-95 on VA 3). Built in 1844, this church was used as a field hospital. Grounds open free daily.

The Stonewall Jackson Memorial Shrine (12 miles south of the park on I-95 to the Thornburg exit, then 5 miles east

55

on VA 606). General Jackson, while on reconnaissance in front of his lines at dusk, was shot by accident by his own men. Ill with pneumonia and with his left arm amputated, he died eight days later, on May 10, 1863.

Open, free, 9 to 5 daily mid-June through Labor Day; Friday through Tuesday, April through mid-June and after Labor Day through October; Saturday through Monday during the rest of the year.

Front Royal

Once known as "Helltown," from the brawls that occurred in the numerous taverns here, Front Royal acquired its present name during the French and Indian War. A frustrated British officer, trying to get his green recruits to line up properly, ordered them to "Front the Royal Oak" growing in the public square. Through repeated use the command was shortened to "Front Royal," from which the town took its name.

The Fall Festival of Leaves, a popular annual attraction, is held here in October. In addition to the spectacular colors of the fall foliage in the Shenandoah National Park and along the Skyline Drive (the entrance is one mile south of Front Royal), there are arts and crafts shows, a parade and beauty pageant, a reenactment of a Civil War battle, and numerous other local activities. For information, write: Chamber of Commerce, 501 S. Royal Ave., Front Royal, VA 22630, or phone (703) 635-3185.

Skyline Caverns (1 mile south of Front Royal on U.S. 340). Discovered in 1937, these caverns are said to be 700 million years old at their deepest point. They are famous for their delicate white anthodite formations, said to be found nowhere else in the world, with a growth estimated at only one inch every 7,000 years. Thirty-seven-foot Rainbow Falls, numerous limestone formations, and a trout stream are among the other sites along the one-hour guided walking tour.

Outside the caverns you can take the miniature Skyline Arrow train ride along a half-mile mountain route. The train operates March through mid-November, weather permitting. Nominal charge.

Open 8:30 to 6:30 Saturday before Memorial Day through Labor Day; 9 to 4:30 Monday following last weekend in October through Thursday before Easter; 9 to 5:30 the rest of the year; last tour begins half an hour before closing. Closed Christmas Day. Admission charge. Picnic area.

Sky Meadows State Park (20 miles east of Front Royal on U.S. 66, then 7 miles north on VA 17). This park of more than 1,000 acres offers picnicking, hiking, and a Visitor Center.

Admission charge.

Thunderbird Museum and Archeological Park (7 miles south of Front Royal, off U.S. 340, on Route 737). The history of man in the Shenandoah Valley is the major focus of this museum, with artifacts dating back more than 11,000 years. During the summer season, visitors are allowed to watch archaeologists at work in nearby excavation areas and hear an explanation of the work in progress. The park's 86 acres in the Blue Ridge Mountains offer more than three miles of nature trails for hikers

Open daily 10 to 5, March 15 through November 15. Admission charge. Picnic area. Craft shop.

Warren Rifles Confederate Museum (95 Chester St.). Civil War relics on display here include uniforms, flags, cavalry equipment, documents, and photographs. There are items that once belonged to such famous figures as generals Jackson, Lee, Longstreet, and Early as well as to Mosley's Rangers. Front Royal was also the home of the beautiful blonde Confederate spy Belle Boyd. In 1862 she passed along information to General Jackson that led to the capture of most of the Union forces under the command of Gen. Nathaniel Banks.

Open daily 9 to 6, April 15 through October; Sundays 12 to 6. Admission charge.

Hampton

Hampton is America's oldest continuous English-speaking settlement. It was founded in 1610 as the town of Kecoughtan, from the name of an Indian village where the first English settlers were welcomed to Hampton's shores.

During the War of 1812, the British pillaged the town and then sailed up the unprotected Chesapeake Bay to capture Washington. As part of a new system of coastal defense, the United States government authorized the construction of Fort Monroe, the largest stone fort ever built in the country; it has been continuously occupied since 1823. The city was devastated once again during the Civil War, when it was burned by Confederate forces to prevent it from falling into Union hands.

Airpower Museum (413 W. Mercury Blvd., U.S. 258). This museum features an "aerospace playground" with authentic jet aircraft, rockets, missiles, and a satellite.

Open free daily.

Bluebird Gap Farm (60 Pine Chapel Rd.). In this unique zoo of candy-striped barns and barnyard animals, city children can become acquainted with farm life.

Open free 9 to 5 Wednesday through Sunday. Closed Thanksgiving, Christmas, and New Year's Day. Playground and picnic area.

Fort Monroe Casemate Museum (at Fort Monroe, Old Point Comfort, 3 miles southeast of Hampton). Robert E. Lee, as an engineer in the United States Army, assisted in the building of Fort Monroe, begun in 1819 and completed in 1834. Shaped like a seven-pointed star and surrounded by a water-filled moat, the stone fort commands the entrance to the world's largest natural harbor, Hampton Roads. Today, it is the only moat-encircled fort still used by the Army, and the installation is the headquarters for the Army Training and Doctrine Command.

Three casemates (chambers in the wall of a fort) have been converted into a museum. In 1865, when he was president of the Confederate States, Jefferson Davis was jailed here for five months after being falsely accused of plotting the assassination of Abraham Lincoln. President Lincoln's successor, Andrew Johnson, charged Davis with the murder and offered a reward of $100,000 for his capture. Davis, his wife and children, and a few loyal followers were captured near Irwinville, Georgia, on May 10, 1865. The cell where Davis was brought and imprisoned after his capture is furnished from details of a sketch left by one of his guards, and a glass case contains some of Davis's personal belongings and the cell lock and key.

Another section of the museum is devoted to displays of the historic battle between the U.S.S. *Monitor* and the *Merrimac*, which occurred within view of the fort. Battle maps, scale models of the ships, ship relics, and a written eyewitness account of the battle by one of the crewmen aboard the *Monitor* tell the fascinating story of this naval encounter.

General McClellan landed his Army of the Potomac at Fort Monroe in 1862 on his way to capture Richmond. Abraham Lincoln came the same year to help plan the attack on Norfolk, and it was here that Lieut. Gen. U. S. Grant planned the strategy that was to win the Civil War. Edgar Allan Poe, one of Fort Monroe's most famous enlisted men, rose to the rank of sergeant-major, the highest rank an enlisted man could attain. Some of his letters are on display, as well as a reproduction of his service uniform.

The first artillery school in America was established here in 1824, and the museum also serves as the Army's Coast Artillery Museum. Some of the armament are displayed around the installation, including the 49,000-pound Lincoln Gun that overlooks the parade field.

Open, free, 10:30 to 5 daily. Closed Thanksgiving, Christmas, and New Year's Day. Gift shop.

Fort Wool (at the mouth of Hampton Roads Harbor, 1 mile south of Fort Monroe). Boat tours make several stops at Fort Wool regularly. Built in 1819, this island fort was visited by Lafayette in 1824. Lieut. Robert E. Lee directed work at the site in 1834. Three presidents spent some time here—Andrew Jackson used the fort as a retreat, John Tyler secluded himself here after the death of his first wife, and

Abraham Lincoln watched from the ramparts here as the Federal fleet attempted to capture Norfolk. Fort Wool was abandoned by the Army in 1967.

Cruise boat schedules are available from the Hampton Information Center, or write: Hampton Roads Cruises, P.O. Box 278, Hampton, VA 23669, or phone (804) 728-0028. Cruise boats also leave from dock at Hampton Tourist Information Center, 710 Settler's Landing Rd., Hampton, phone (804) 727-6108.

Hampton Harbor Tours (at Joseph E. Healy, Jr., Memorial Park on Settler's Landing Road). Tour boats cruise through the headquarters of the U.S. Atlantic fleet at Hampton Roads, past huge merchant vessels and ships of war, through waters once terrorized by Blackbeard the Pirate, under the ramparts of Fort Monroe, and past the site of the battles of the *Monitor* and the *Merrimac*.

For a schedule and fees, write: Hampton Harbor Tours, 530 12th St., Newport News, VA 23607, or phone (804) 245-1533. Snack bar aboard.

Hampton University (East Queen Street). This institute of higher learning was founded in 1868 to provide for the education of freed slaves after the Civil War. Booker T. Washington, founder of Tuskegee Institute in Alabama, was an alumnus. Many Indians were educated here between 1878 and 1923. Hampton University is now a modern liberal arts college, with many of the buildings originally built by the freedmen still in use today.

A museum on the campus displays numerous collections, including American Indian, African, fine art, Asian and Oceanic, and a wide variety of objects relating to the history of Hampton University.

Museum open, free, daily. Closed mid-December to early January.

Kecoughtan Indian Village (418 W. Mercury Blvd.). This village is a reproduction of the type lived in by the Kecoughtan Indians, who befriended the English settlers when they established a settlement in Hampton more than 350 years ago.

Open free daily. Closed major holidays.

N.A.S.A. Langley Research Center (3 miles north of Hampton on VA 134). The astronauts trained here for the Apollo 11 moon shot. The Visitor Center has a film and numerous aeronautical exhibits, including David Scott's space suit, the Apollo 12 Command Module, and a lunar rock.

Open, free, 8:30 to 4:30 daily, 12 to 4:30 Sunday. Closed Easter, Thanksgiving, Christmas, and New Year's Day. Picnic area, gift shop.

St. John's Episcopal Church (100 W. Queens Way). Established in 1610, built in 1728, this Episcopal parish is the oldest English-speaking parish in continuous service in America. In 1812 British troops were quartered here. The church boasts communion silver dating from 1618, a Vestry book dated 1751-84, a Breeches Bible printed in 1599, and a Prayer Book of 1637.

Open 8 to 4 daily, and for 10 A.M. Thursday morning and 8 A.M. and 10 A.M. Sunday services.

Syms-Eaton Museum (418 W. Mercury Blvd.). This museum is named for Benjamin Syms and Thomas Eaton who, in 1634 and 1659, founded the first free public schools in America, established for the poor children of the parish. Historical exhibits and displays depict the history of Hampton, beginning with the arrival of the English settlers in 1607. A popular exhibit is the 1800s schoolroom with potbellied stove and old wooden desks.

Free, open 8 to 5 Wednesday through Friday, 10 to 5 Saturday and Sunday. Closed major holidays.

Hanover

Hanover Courthouse. Patrick Henry first gained prominence in this courthouse in 1763 in a legal case he pleaded called *The Parson's Cause,* a dispute involving clerical salaries. The building is still used as a courthouse.

Hanover Tavern (13 miles north of Richmond, on U.S. 301, across the street from the Courthouse). Hanover Tavern was built in 1723, nine years before George Washington was born. The tavern owner's daughter, Sarah Shelton, married

Patrick Henry. He lived here for a time, and occasionally served as host in his father-in-law's absence. For two weeks in 1781 Hanover Tavern was the headquarters of Lord Cornwallis and Colonel Tarleton, on their way to attack Yorktown, where they were defeated. Other famous visitors were Jefferson, Benjamin Franklin, Washington, and Lafayette.

The tavern now serves as the Barksdale Theatre, the oldest dinner theatre in the country. Performances year round, Wednesday through Saturday, 8:30 P.M. Dinner optional, by reservation only, 6:45 to 8 P.M. For reservations phone (804) 537-5333.

Harrisonburg

This is the main gateway to the George Washington National Forest (10 miles west of Harrisonburg on U.S. 33) and the Shenandoah National Park (24 miles east on U.S. 33). There are miles of horseback and hiking trails, scenic drives, big- and small-game hunting, camping, picnicking, and swimming areas. The Shenandoah River and Lake Shenandoah (3 miles east) are famous for their trout and bass fishing. Harrisonburg is the seat of Rockingham County, well known as the nation's Turkey Capital, with an annual production of more than 5 million turkeys.

Displays of Shenandoah Valley history can be seen at the Harrisonburg-Rockingham Historical Society, 301 S. Main St.

This is also the site of James Madison University, on S. Main Street, with campus tours available at the Admissions Office, and of the Eastern Mennonite College and Seminary (for campus tours, phone (703) 433-2771).

For more information, contact the Harrisonburg-Rockingham Chamber of Commerce, 191 S. Main St., P.O. Box 1, Harrisonburg, VA 22801, or phone (703) 434-3862.

Grand Caverns (12 miles south of Harrisonburg on I-81, then 6 miles east on VA 256 in Grottoes). Located in the Shenandoah Valley, these caverns, the first discovered in Virginia, were found in 1804. They have been visited by Thomas Jefferson and used by Stonewall Jackson to hold religious services and to quarter his troops and horses during the Civil War. In addition to their unusual formations, the caverns are famous for the 5,000-square-foot room known as the Grand Ballroom, once the site of many antebellum balls. There is a one-hour guided tour leaving every 30 minutes.

Nearby are tennis courts, a swimming pool, hiking and bicycle trails, a miniature golf course, and picnic areas in the Grand Caverns Regional Park.

Open daily 9 to 5 April to October; weekends only in March. Admission charge.

Lincoln Homestead (9 miles north of Harrisonburg on VA 42). The rear wing of this house was built by the grandfather of Abraham Lincoln; it was here that Lincoln's father was born.

Private residence, not open to the public.

Massanutten Caverns (2 1/2 miles north of U.S. 33 in Keezletown). These caverns of unusual limestone formations were discovered in 1892. Guided tours.

Open daily spring to fall; weekends only in winter. Schedule changes yearly, phone (703) 269-6555. Admission charge.

Natural Chimneys (15 miles southwest of Harrisonburg off VA 42 in Mount Solon). Seven massive limestone columns rising 120 feet—named for their resemblance to the furnaces used to smelt iron prior to the Civil War—comprise this unusual attraction. Shallow tunnels were carved out of the base of the 500 million-year-old formations by the water action of an ancient underground stream; at the top of the columns are intrusions from old lava flows. One of the "chimneys" has the added interest of leaning at 13 1/2 feet from the perpendicular, at about the same angle as the Leaning Tower of Pisa.

Interpretive recordings and drawings give the history of the formation of the limestone columns. Their resemblance to medieval turrets and towers inspired settlers in 1821 to hold a medieval jousting tournament at this location, a tradition which has continued, making it the oldest continuously held sporting event in America. The tournaments are held annually on the third Saturday in August.

The area also offers a gift shop, wooded picnic areas, seasonal swimming at an Olympic-size swimming pool, hiking and bicycle trails, a playground, and 120 level camping sites and limited camping facilities open December 1 to March 1. Park open daily 9 A.M. to dark. Admission charge. Camping reservations suggested; phone (703) 350-2510.

George Washington National Forest (10 miles west of Harrisonburg on U.S. 33). George Washington National Forest covers more than a million acres in three separate sections along the Blue Ridge, Shenandoah Mountains, and Massanutten mountain areas. These scenic forestlands have well-developed public recreation areas, woodland drives, hundreds of miles of hiking and horseback trails, and accommodations for thousands of campers. Fishing is excellent, with miles of streams well stocked with trout, bass, and bluegill. Hunting for white-tailed deer, wild turkey, black bear, and smaller game is plentiful here, the largest public hunting ground in the East. Scenic natural features provide interesting stops at falls, caverns and caves, and unusual rock formations.

The Massanutten Visitor Center (between New Market and Luray on U.S. 211) is open early spring through late fall. For additional information, write: Forest Supervisor, Harrison Plaza, P.O. Box 233, Harrisonburg, VA 22801, or phone (703) 433-2491.

Hopewell

Flowerdew Hundred (10 miles southeast of Hopewell on VA 10). Archaeological excavations here (summers) are revealing finds dating back to the prehistoric period. Many relics are on display in the museum.

Open Tuesday through Sunday, April through November. Admission charge. Visitor Center, 18th-century windmill (still in operation), bookstore, gift shop. Picnic area.

Merchants Hope Church (6 miles east of Hopewell on VA 10, then 1/2 mile south on VA 641). This 1657 church has been praised for its exterior colonial brickwork, called the most beautiful in the nation. It is the oldest Protestant church still standing in the country.

Weston Manor (N. 21st Avenue, on Appomattox River). The land here was originally occupied by the Appomatuck Indian tribe, whose queen welcomed Capt. Christopher Newport and his exploration party shortly after the settlement of Jamestown, 30 miles downstream.

Weston Manor's proximity to the Appomattox River also thrust the home into the historical scenes of the Civil War. Gen. Philip Sheridan and his officers used the house as their headquarters and left behind a permanent record of their visit when they scratched their names into a glass windowpane. Before the Federal troops took over the house, they shelled it from a gunboat on the river below. One of the cannonballs sailed through a dining-room window and struck the ceiling, where it remained until it was accidentally dislodged during restoration. The cannonball has been preserved and placed on display.

Also of interest are the doors in the house. After the Civil War the owners took them down and rehung them from the left side, "to drive out evil spirits and ghosts."

Open daily, by appointment only; phone (804) 458-4862. Admission charge.

Hot Springs

Homestead Ski Area and Resorts (on U.S. 220). Snow-skiing facilities here include equipment rentals, professional instruction, ski patrol, and chair and rope lifts. For more information, phone (703) 839-5079.

Open 9 to 5 daily November through March.

The Cascades Inn (3 miles south of Hot Springs on VA 220). The inn offers hotel, motel, and cottage facilities at the scenic Cascades gorge.

Open daily April through October. For more information, phone (703) 839-5355.

The Homestead resort facilities include hotel rooms and cottages, Olympic-size pool, pro golf instruction at three 18-

hole golf courses, tennis, skeet and trap shooting, bowling, carriage drives, dancing, movies, concerts, spa, and mineral pool. An Olympic-size ice-skating rink is open mid-November through March. Luncheon buffets and box luncheons available. Airstrip adjacent to resort.

Open April through October. For more information, phone (703) 839-5500.

Irvington

The Tides Inn (1/4 mile south of Irvington on VA 3). This resort hotel is set in a hillside and has a scenic water view. Recreational facilities include an Olympic-size saltwater pool, golfing, lighted tennis, bicycling, sailing, boating, waterskiing, dancing, movies, and recreation room. Ferry service across a creek goes to the Golf Lodge hotel (open mid-March through late November). Transportation by nearby bus depot, airport, and railroad.

For sightseeing information, see *Lancaster County.*

Resort open daily mid-March through December. For reservations, phone (800) 843-3746; for more information, call (804) 438-5000.

Jamestown

Jamestown (10 miles from Williamsburg via the Colonial Parkway). Often called "the most historic spot in the nation," Jamestown is the site of the first permanent English settlement in America. On April 26, 1607, the 104 settlers aboard the *Susan Constant,* the *Godspeed,* and the *Discovery* landed at Cape Henry and erected a wooden cross to give thanks for a safe voyage after a wintry crossing. On May 13, 1607, they landed on what was then an island in the James River and established the colony of Jamestown.

Although additional settlers arrived, the tiny colony suffered greatly from hunger, sickness, Indian attacks, and disease. The terrible "Starving Time" in the winter of 1609 saw the population shrink from more than 500 to about 60 persons. The remaining colonists voted to abandon the settlement, but when Lord De La Warr arrived in June with 150 new settlers and provisions, they decided to stay, and the colony was saved.

The gold that the investors in the Virginia Company had hoped for was not found, but the discovery of a new way to cure tobacco caused a rapid expansion of settlement along the James River and brought prosperity to Jamestown. In 1620 the Virginia Company sent women to the all-male colony to bring stability and permanence to the settlement. By 1622 the population had grown to about 1,250.

The day the English landed at Cape Henry they were attacked by Indians, and through the years such success as the colonists had with the Indians was due largely to the friendship of Chief Powhatan's young daughter, Pocahontas. When only 13 years old, she pleaded on behalf of John Smith and saved him from the death her father had ordered. She frequently visited Jamestown, was baptized in the Christian faith, and in 1614 married John Rolfe and went with him to England. In 1622, just five years after her death, the Indians rose up and massacred 347 settlers, about one-fourth of the colony's population. Jamestown was saved only because it had been forewarned by a friendly Indian youth.

Political problems also plagued the colony. The royal governor, Lord Berkeley, was disliked by the citizens, who felt that they were not being given enough protection from the Indians. A group of colonists led by Nathaniel Bacon, Jr., defied Berkeley and led an expedition against the Indians. Governor Berkeley condemned the action and declared Bacon and his followers outlaws and traitors. In 1676 Bacon led an expedition into Jamestown, where he captured the city and burned it to the ground, forcing Berkeley to flee. The rebellion ended when Bacon became ill and died, leaving his followers without a leader.

The State House was rebuilt, but it burned again for the fourth time in 1698, and the decision was made to move Virginia's capital to Williamsburg, six miles inland. From that time on Jamestown declined. By the beginning of the American Revolution, the town had almost completely died out, with practically nothing but the foundations left, even the bricks having been hauled away to help build Williamsburg.

The only standing ruin from 17th-century Jamestown is the tower of the old 1639 church, built on the site of the first legislative assembly of 1619.

In 1934 archaeologists uncovered the original foundations of the town, reopening streets, marking off property lines, and exposing 17th-century foundations. Interpretive markers, paintings, and recordings aid the visitor in visualizing Jamestown as it was when it was a small colony struggling to survive in the New World. A statue of Capt. John Smith faces James River at the site of his landing, and a wooden cross erected in memory of the 440 settlers who died in the severe winter of 1609-10 marks the earliest known burying ground of men and women in America.

At the visitors' parking lot, there is a short trail first used by colonists to go from Jamestown Island to the mainland. The trail leads to a reconstructed 1608 Glasshouse—the site of America's first industry—where glass is blown as it was by colonial craftsmen. Visitors can purchase these reproductions of early ware.

A modern Visitor Center has free brochures, exhibits, and a post office. Free; open daily 9 to 6 mid-June through Labor Day, 8:30 to 5:30 after Labor Day through October and April through mid-June; 9 to 5 November through March. Closed Christmas Day. Park Entrance Station open daily 8:30 to 5:30 mid-June through Labor Day, to 5 P.M. after Labor Day through October and April through mid-June; to 4:30 November through March. Closed Christmas Day. Vehicle admission charge. Cafe.

Colonial National Historical Parkway. This scenic, 23-mile drive along the James and York rivers and adjoining woodlands links three of America's most important historical sites and over 350 years of history. The drive follows the shores of the James River along the water route traveled by the *Susan Constant*, the *Godspeed*, and the *Discovery* in 1607 to reach Jamestown. Approaching Yorktown, the parkway passes American and French siege points, with gun emplacements aimed towards Cornwallis's defense points.

The parkway begins at the Visitor Center at Jamestown, the site of the first permanent English settlement in 1607;

borders the Information Center at Williamsburg, the 18th-century capital; and ends at the Information Center in Yorktown, where American independence was won in 1781. All the exhibits along the drive are open throughout the year. Parkway free to private vehicles; 45 mph speed limit; no service stations; picnic areas.

Jamestown Ferry Boat (on Route 31 near Jamestown). Whether bound for the Bacon's Castle area or for Jamestown, plan to take this ferryboat across the James River. During the crossing, passengers are permitted to go topside to view the James River shores where the colonists landed in 1607.

Runs daily on the hour and the half-hour, from 6 A.M. to 11:30 P.M. (Times may vary.) Vehicle charge.

Jamestown Festival Park (1 mile from Jamestown, adjoining the Colonial Parkway and Route 31). History comes alive at Jamestown Festival Park, where displays and exhibits re-create the colorful story of America's first permanent English settlement. A modern arcade of buildings houses the Old World Heritage Exhibit and the New World Achievement Exhibit. Dioramas, works of art, historic maps, models, and priceless relics (such as the cameo presented to Pocahontas by the court of England in 1617) portray the events and achievements of Virginia and her people from the settlement of Jamestown to the present.

During the walking tour visitors can view full-sized reproductions of an Indian ceremonial lodge, pottery, fort, and the ships that brought the first settlers to Jamestown. The Indian lodge, measuring 36 feet long and 16 feet wide, is representative of those lived in by the Indians when the first settlers arrived. Nearby is a dance circle of six-foot poles topped by carved heads, and a "scarecrow's hut" where the old men of the tribe kept watch over planted fields and frightened away birds with gourd rattles. Descendants of the Indians who met the settlers in 1607, dressed in their native costumes, greet visitors and answer questions about Indian life in colonial days.

A reproduction of a 17th-century pottery, one of the first industries in Jamestown, has artisans at work making replicas of colonial wares. The clay is taken from the banks of the James River, just as it was centuries ago, and the finished pottery is offered for sale in the gift shop.

When the settlers went ashore on May 14, 1607, they began to build a log fort for protection against the Indians and Spaniards. James Fort has been authentically reproduced, complete with ship's guns mounted in the bulwarks. The 18 buildings inside the fort contain period furnishings. June through August, costumed attendants perform colonial chores, haberdiers in 17th-century armor perform hourly changing-of-the-guard ceremonies, and historical lectures are given in the fort's church, a replica of the one built in 1610.

At the edge of the James River are full-scale reproductions of the *Discovery, Godspeed,* and *Susan Constant,* the ships that brought the first settlers to Jamestown. Visitors are allowed to board the *Susan* and inspect its narrow, cramped quarters.

Open daily 9 to 5; hours are extended mid-June to mid-August; closed Christmas and New Year's Day. Admission charge. Picnic area, snack bar.

Lancaster County

Epping Forest (11 miles above Kilmarnock; 4 miles west of Lancaster, on VA 3). In 1708, Mary Ball Washington, the mother of George Washington, was born in this home. Still a working plantation, it has four of the original outbuildings—the coach house, smokehouse, laundry, and unique icehouse, 25 feet deep and lined with 15,000 handmade bricks using absolutely no mortar. The house itself is beautifully preserved and even contains some of the original glass panes.

Open daily 9 to 5, April through November. Admission charge.

Historic Christ Church (off VA 3, above Irvington on Route 646). Built in 1732, the year George Washington was born, this church has been described as "the most perfect example of colonial church architecture now remaining in Virginia." The church stands virtually unchanged today, with the original three-decker pulpit and "sounding board" (to carry the minister's voice to the back of the church), limestone paving in the aisles, and high-backed pews, the only original ones of the period remaining in Virginia's churches. On display is the church's original communion silver, Queen Anne holy table, and communion rail.

Inside the church is a 1674 tomb and—under a slab in the chancel—the graves of John Carter and four of his five wives. The church was erected on the site of an earlier wooden church, and its construction was financed by Robert ("King") Carter, agent for Lord Fairfax and wealthy plantation owner, so that the graves of his parents could remain in the chancel.

In the graveyard outside are the tombs of Robert Carter and his two wives, who count among their distinguished descendants eight governors of Virginia, three signers of the Declaration of Independence, two presidents of the United States, Gen. Robert E. Lee, and one chief justice of the Supreme Court.

Free; open daily 9 to 5; closed Christmas Day.

The Carter Reception Center and museum are open from April through Thanksgiving with guided tours from 10 to 4 Monday through Friday, 1 to 4 Saturdays, and 2 to 5 Sundays.

Lancaster Courthouse (on VA 3). The Court House Green includes the original clerk's office (1797), colonial jail, and courthouse (1863). Lancaster House (1798) on the Court House Green contains the Mary Ball Washington Museum and Library. George Washington's mother, Mary Ball, was born in Lancaster County. She and her family worshiped here at St. Mary's White Church, and many tombstones bear the Ball name.

Open, free, 10 A.M. to 4 P.M. Tuesday through Friday. Closed all major holidays.

Leesburg

Originally named Georgetown, for King George of England, Leesburg changed its name in honor of a local landowner, Francis Lightfoot Lee, who later became one of the signers of the Declaration of Independence.

During the War of 1812, when Washington, D.C., was in flames, President Madison and his cabinet fled here to escape capture by the British. They took with them 22 wagonloads of government documents, including the Constitution and the Declaration of Independence, which they entrusted to the safekeeping of Rev. John Littlejohn, minister of the local Methodist Episcopal Church. This church, still standing today, is part of the walking tour of the town. Information about the tour is available at the Visitor's Center, 108-D South St. SE; phone (703) 777-0519.

American Work Horse Museum (4 miles west of Leesburg via VA 7 on Route 662). Equestrian equipment, blacksmith tools, veterinary supplies, and everything related to the work horse and its early role in the settlement of our country is on display in this museum.

Open, free, Wednesdays April through October.

Balls Bluff (north of Leesburg on U.S. 15). This is the smallest national cemetery in the country. It was the site of a battle during the Civil War where Oliver Wendell Holmes, Jr., who later became a U.S. Supreme Court justice, was wounded.

Open free daily.

Hill High Orchards (15 miles west of Leesburg on VA 7). Visitors can enjoy picking their own apples, peaches, and strawberries (in season). Home-baked pies and other goods are offered for sale.

Open free daily. Closed Christmas and New Year's Day. For information about activities, phone (703) 338-7173.

Laurel Brigade Inn (on VA 7, 20 W. Market St.). This cozy 1766 inn was used by President James Monroe in 1825 to entertain the Marquis de Lafayette. There are a few overnight rooms, "Colonial cooking for the Gentle Palate," antique furnishings, and a small garden to stroll in. Nearby is the Loudoun Museum.

Lunch served 12 to 2; dinner 5:30 to 8:30; Friday and Saturday to 9; open Sunday 12 to 7. Closed Mondays,

Christmas Day, and January to mid-February. For reservations phone (703) 777-1010.

Loudoun County Museum (16 W. Loudoun St.). This building was originally a silversmith's shop, built about 1767. The museum is now filled with unique historical keepsakes, including a china teapot belonging to Dolley Madison, with a lid that is a miniature copy of her favorite hat; a snuffbox that General Lafayette gave his dancing partner at a ball here in 1825; a letter from Lord Loudoun (the county was named in his honor) dated April 20, 1762; a pair of vases made by the personal jeweler of Louis XV; an original deed of property signed by George Washington, dated November 1, 1774; and a black gown belonging to Mrs. Abraham Lincoln.

Free; open 10 to 5, Monday through Saturday; 1 to 5 Sunday. Closed Thanksgiving, Christmas, and New Year's Day.

Morven Park (west on North Street, then north on Old Waterford Road). This 1,200-acre estate has been the home of two governors, Westmoreland Davis of Virginia and Thomas Swann of Maryland. The mansion is fronted with a spectacular garden of horticultural exhibits, and brochures guide visitors who wish to follow the nature trails. Also on the grounds is the Carriage Museum housing 125 horse-drawn vehicles, from simple wagons and luxurious coaches to sleighs of all shapes and sizes.

The 16 rooms of the mansion open to the public are lavishly appointed with hand-carved antique furniture, oriental rugs, family portraits, rich chandeliers, and artifacts collected by Governor and Mrs. Davis on their extensive travels in Europe and Asia. The Great Hall or Renaissance Room is hung with four huge tapestries woven in Flanders during the 16th century.

Open Tuesday through Saturday and holiday Mondays Memorial Day to Labor Day; weekends May to October. Admission charge.

Mountain Gap School (4 miles south of Leesburg on Route 15). Built in 1885, this restored one-room schoolhouse shows visitors what education was like before the turn of the century.

Open irregularly, on special holidays. (For further information, contact the Loudoun County Chamber of Commerce.)

Oatlands (6 miles south of Leesburg on U.S. 15). Oatlands was built between 1800 and 1803 by George Carter, great-grandson of famed Virginia planter Robert ("King") Carter. The 13-room mansion was once the center of a thriving 5,000-acre plantation, but with the Civil War the fortunes of the prestigious Carter family were considerably diminished. Confederate troops were quartered in the house, and in the late 1880s the Carters were forced to sell some of their furnishings and land and take in boarders.

Today the estate is restored to its former splendor, with ornate cornicework, family portraits, many original furnishings, and antiques from America, England, and France. The formal gardens, with their renowned boxwood collection, were planted and designed by George Carter, who lies here in the family tomb.

Annual events include the Loudoun Hunt point-to-point races and a horse and foxhound show in April, and the Hunter Trials in late autumn. Needlework exhibits are held each fall, and the 1800s Yuletide atmosphere of Oatlands is revived each year in mid-November, when decorations of pinecones, laurel, magnolia leaves, fruit, and nuts are arranged throughout the house.

Open daily April to mid-December. Admission charge.

Waterford (3 miles northwest of Leesburg on VA 7, right 1 mile on VA 9, 2 miles north on VA 662). Pennsylvania Quakers established this picturesque community in the early part of the 18th century, and by 1834 it was a flourishing village with several factories. It remained closely tied to its Pennsylvania heritage, and the sympathies of its villagers were with the Union during the Civil War. The town today is a favorite tourist attraction during the annual Homes Tour and Crafts Exhibit each October, when many historic 18th- and 19th-century homes and buildings are opened to the public, handcrafted articles are offered for sale, and artisans demonstrate early crafts. For more information phone (703) 882-3018.

White's Ferry (4 miles north of Leesburg off Route 15 on Route 655). This ferryboat is the last still in operation on the Potomac. During the Civil War, generals Robert E. Lee and Jeb Stuart crossed here with their armies.

Open 6 A.M. to 11 P.M. Runs every 15 minutes. Vehicle charge.

Lexington

This historic town, established in 1777, counts among its famous residents the Confederate leaders Robert E. Lee and Stonewall Jackson, both buried here, and World War II Chief of Staff George C. Marshall, a graduate of the Virginia Military Institute. Lexington is the seat of Rockbridge County, birthplace of Samuel Houston and Cyrus McCormick, inventor of the grain reaper (see *Staunton*). Two of the state's foremost educational institutions, the Virginia Military Institute and Washington and Lee University, are part of the tours of the town. For information, stop at the Visitor Information Center, 102 E. Washington St., or phone (703) 463-3777.

Henry Street Playhouse (on Henry Street in historic downtown district). This summer-stock playhouse offers musicals and melodramas in a turn-of-the-century atmosphere.

Open mid-June through mid-August, Wednesday through Saturday, 8 P.M.; Sunday matinee 2 P.M. For information write: Henry Street Playhouse, P.O. Box 1087, Lexington, VA 24450, or phone (703) 463-8637.

Stonewall Jackson House (8 E. Washington St.). The only house ever owned by Confederate general Stonewall Jackson, this was his residence for three years until he went off to war, never to return. The house is authentically furnished with family possessions and personal items belonging to Jackson. He is buried in Lexington's Jackson Memorial Cemetery, located on the east side of Main Street.

Open daily 9 to 4:30, Monday through Saturday, 1 to 4:30 Sunday. Closed Easter, Thanksgiving, Christmas, and New Year's Day. Admission charge.

Lee Chapel (on the campus of Washington and Lee University). Lee Chapel was built under Robert E. Lee's supervision while he served as president of Washington College (from 1865 until his death in 1870). After Lee's death the chapel was enlarged to accommodate family tombs of the Lees dating from Revolutionary times. The chapel contains a famous recumbent marble statue of General Lee by Valentine, a museum housing the Washington and Lee families' art collection, and the office of General Lee, furnished just as he left it.

Free; open 9 to 5 Monday through Saturday, mid-April through mid-October; rest of year to 4 P.M.; 2 to 5 Sundays all year. Closed Thanksgiving and the following Friday, December 24–26 and 31, and New Year's Day.

George C. Marshall Research Library and Museum (on the west edge of the Virginia Military Institute Parade Ground). Built on the campus from which he graduated in 1901, this impressive memorial to George C. Marshall traces his career from his service as a young cadet to Army chief of staff in World War II, ambassador to China, secretary of state, secretary of defense, and architect of the European Recovery Program, popularly known as the Marshall Plan. Among his many honors was the coveted Nobel Peace Prize, awarded in 1953, on display in the museum. Exhibits also include a collection of personal flags, family articles, and an entire room of murals and displays devoted to explaining the purpose and achievements of the Marshall Plan. A World War II "talking map" utilizes moving lights and a recorded narrative to trace the main events of the Second World War. The library contains thousands of General Marshall's personal papers, military and diplomatic documents, photographs, and maps.

General Marshall died October 16, 1959; he is buried at Arlington National Cemetery.

Free, open 9 to 5 Monday through Saturday, 2 to 5 Sunday; closes at 4 P.M. from mid-October through mid-April. Closed Easter, Thanksgiving, Christmas, and New Year's Day.

Virginia Military Institute and V.M.I. Museum (off N. Main Street, U.S. 11, on Letcher Avenue). Founded in 1839 to produce "citizen-soldiers," this college has produced such outstanding military leaders as generals Stonewall Jackson, George Patton, and George C. Marshall. Gen. Stonewall Jackson was a professor at V.M.I. for ten years, teaching natural and experimental philosophy and artillery tactics until the outbreak of the Civil War.

Visitors may watch the Dress Parades each Friday, September through May, at 4:15 P.M. and the Guard Mount daily September through May at 12:30 P.M., weather permitting.

The V.M.I. Museum, located in Jackson Memorial Hall, tells the history of the college and the achievements of its graduates.

Free; open 9 to 4:30 Monday through Friday, 9 to 12 Saturday, and 2 to 5 Sunday. Closed Easter, Thanksgiving, December 24-31, and New Year's Day.

For the story of the cadet charge at the Battle of New Market in 1864, see *New Market Battlefield Park, New Market.*

Washington and Lee University (S. Jefferson and W. Washington streets). Founded in 1749 as Augusta Academy, this is the nation's sixth oldest college. It became Washington College in 1872, named in Washington's honor for his endowment gift of $50,000. Robert E. Lee served as president of the college after the Civil War, and at his death in 1870 his name was added.

Lincoln

This picturesque Quaker community (off Route 7 from Purcellville) was settled prior to 1740. Originally it was named Goose Creek, but later the name was changed in honor of President Abraham Lincoln. It still resembles an early Quaker village, with many restored 18th-century homes, farmhouses, and other early structures. Stony Lonesome (not open to tours) was constructed in 1790 of native fieldstone and is bordered by ancient trees and stone fences.

Luray

For a look at an old homestead town and a sampling of our early American heritage, visit Luray in October when the community joins together to stage its annual Page County

Heritage Festival. Craft demonstrations, covered-wagon rides, square dances, cider-making, and sorghum-molasses and apple-butter boilings are just part of the fun. Many historic churches and homes are opened for tours. Some of these early homes, built to guard against the constant threat of Indian attacks, contain thick stone forts built within their walls, usually in the basement. These forts were kept stocked with food and firewood and often had a tunnel leading to a well above the waterline to serve as a source of water.

For information, write: Luray Chamber of Commerce, 46 E. Main St., Luray, VA 22835, or phone (703) 743-3915.

Luray Caverns (west edge of town on U.S. 211, between Skyline Drive and I-81). Cool air coming from a sinkhole led to the discovery of Luray Caverns in 1878. The one-hour guided tour follows wide, brick-paved corridors past massive limestone formations and mirrorlike pools of water. The cavern's "Great Stalacpipe Organ," an organ that produces music from the different shapes and positions of the stalactites instead of from pipes, is played for visitors. This is the world's largest musical instrument, covering 64 acres.

Ticketholders may also see the Historic Car and Carriage Caravan, exhibiting an 1892 Benz, 1906 Ford, 1907 Buick, 1911 Hupmobile, 1913 Stanley Steamer, and Rudolph Valentino's 1925 Rolls Royce.

One mile west of the caverns is the Caverns Country Club, with four tennis courts and an 18-hole golf course. For golf and tennis package plans, phone (703) 743-6551 daily from 9 till 5. Private plane fly-in at Luray Caverns Airport, 1/2 mile west of the caverns.

Open 9 to 6 March 15 through June 14, 9 to 7 June 15 through Labor Day, 9 to 6 day after Labor Day through November 14, 9 to 4 November 15 through March 14 (9 to 5 Saturdays and Sundays). Tours leave about every 20 minutes. Admission charge. Caverns and Coach Restaurant adjacent to the Caverns entrance building.

Lynchburg

A tobacco-exporting community built up around the ferry service started at the river here in 1757 by 17-year-old John

Lynch, for whom the town was named. He later built what is believed to be the first tobacco warehouse in the country.

During the Civil War, the Confederates kept a supply base here. It was raided on June 18, 1864, by Union forces, but they were beaten off by Rebel troops under the command of General Early. The remains of the earthwork fort where he made his stand can be seen at Fort and Vermont avenues.

Lynchburg today is the home of four institutions of higher learning—Randolph-Macon Woman's College, the first accredited college for women in Virginia, at 2500 Rivermont Ave.; Liberty Baptist College, near the intersection of U.S. 29 and U.S. 460; Lynchburg College, at U.S. 221 on the west edge of the city; and Virginia Seminary and College at Dewitt Street and Garfield Avenue.

For a Visitor's Guide to shopping, factory outlets, dining, night life, lodging, transportation, and historical sites, write: Visitor Center, 12th and Church Streets, P.O. Box 60, Lynchburg, VA 24505, or phone (804) 847-1811.

Blackwater Creek Natural Area (in the city of Lynchburg). This 115-acre preserve offers historical sites of interest, lush hiking trails, bicycle paths, and recreational areas.

Open free daily.

Old Court House Museum (901 Court St.). Three galleries of exhibits of this area's early history are housed here. The building has been restored to its original Greek Revival appearance.

Open Tuesday through Saturday, March through December. Admission charge.

Point of Honor (112 Cabell St.). Named for the many duels fought here, this restored mansion is appointed with early 19th-century furnishings.

Open Tuesday through Saturday, March through December. Closed major holidays. Admission charge.

Poplar Forest (10 miles west of Lynchburg on U.S. 221, then south on VA 661). Thomas Jefferson designed and built this octagonally shaped residence as his summer home.

Open weekends only May through November. Admission charge.

Riverside Park (Rivermont Avenue). This park offers a train ride and historical sites of interest, including the packet boat which carried the remains of Stonewall Jackson to Lexington.
Open free daily.

Anne Spenser House (1317 Pierce St.). This was the residence of the distinguished black female poet and the only Virginian to be included in the renowned *Norton Anthology of Modern American and British Poetry.*
Admission charge. Open by appointment only; phone (804) 846-0517.

Manassas

Manassas City Museum (9406 Main St.). Local and Civil War historical exhibits are displayed in this 1894 National Bank building.
Open free daily. Closed major holidays.

Manassas National Battlefield Park (Bull Run) (at junction of U.S. 29, 211, VA 234). Two great battles of the Civil War—on July 21, 1861 and August 28–30, 1862—were fought on this site, popularly known as Bull Run, from the name of a small stream here. Both were Confederate victories and paved the way for General Lee's invasion of Maryland. In the first battle, the first major clash of the war, the Federals met the resistance of Confederate general Thomas Jonathan Jackson standing "like a stone wall," earning him the nickname "Stonewall" Jackson. The battle forced the Union army to retreat, a rout ending only at the defenses of Washington. In the second battle Gen. Robert E. Lee defeated Union general John Pope's attacking army, which was driven back across Bull Run. In pursuit General Jackson was stopped at Chantilly on September 1, 1862, and Pope withdrew to Washington.

The Manassas Visitor Center (on Henry Hill, north of I-64 off VA 234) presents an audiovisual program, museum of Civil War relics, electric map outlining the battle campaign, and free maps for the self-guided walking tour. Interpretive markers throughout the battlefield give the historical background of the various sites.

On the battlefield, an equestrian statue of Confederate general Jackson marks the place where he earned the nickname "Stonewall." At Stone Bridge the Federals opened the first battle with an artillery barrage. Chinn House Ruins and Stone House, originally a tavern, were used as field hospitals.

The park is open, free, daily 9 to 9 June through September, until dark October through May. Closed Christmas Day.

Visitor Center open, free, daily 9 to 6.

Battlefield Museum in Visitor Center open, free, daily 9 to 6 June 15 through Labor Day, until 5:30 P.M. the rest of the year. Closed Christmas Day.

Marion

Hungry Mother State Park (3 miles north of Marion on VA 16). Fishing, boating (rentals and ramp), swimming, horseback riding, hiking on park nature trails, and picnicking are popular activities in this park of more than 2,000 acres with a 108-acre lake. Camping areas and vacation cabins are available April through November. There is a cafe for meals and snacks, and a Visitor Center with museum presents evening programs.

This is the site of the popular Arts and Crafts Festival (third weekend in July).

Admission charge to certain facilities. For more information, write: Chamber of Commerce, P.O. Box 924, 132 W. Main St., Marion, VA 24354, or phone (703) 783-3161.

Jefferson National Forest. More than 600,000 acres of scenic and recreational areas in this park extend from the James River near Natural Bridge to the southwest tip of Virginia. The area offers camping, hiking, picnicking, and trout fishing, and is famous for its deer, turkey, grouse, and squirrel hunting.

Admission charge to certain facilities. For more information, write: Forest Supervisor, 210 Franklin Rd. S.W., Roanoke, VA 24001, or phone (703) 982-6270. (See also *Breaks Interstate Park*, adjacent to Jefferson National Forest.)

Southeast of Marion via VA 16 is Mount Rogers National Recreation Area; for more information, contact the Marion Chamber of Commerce (above).

Martinsville

Blue Ridge Farm Museum (in Ferrum, on VA 40). Living history programs with costumed interpreters show what farm life was like in the mountains in the 1800s. On the grounds are a log house, kitchen, and barn.
Open weekends only June through August. Admission charge.

Fairy Stone State Park (21 miles northwest via U.S. 220, VA 57, 822). A clear lake and 4,570-acre wooded park offer hiking, horseback riding, bicycling, picnicking, fishing, boat rentals, swimming, and evening programs at the Visitor Center. Cafe and concession; cabins (May through September). Tent and trailer sites (April through November).

Martinsville Speedway Stock Car Races (3 miles south of Martinsville). Several stock car races are held here annually. For more information, write Martinsville Stock Car Races, Box 3311, Martinsville, VA 24112, or phone (703) 956-3151.

Philpott Lake (northeast of Fairy Stone State Park). Philpott Lake was formed by the waters of a dam built by the U.S. Corps of Army Engineers. The fourth largest lake in the state, it offers swimming, boating, fishing, water-skiing, picnicking, hiking on nature trails, and camping (mid-May through mid-September). For information, write: Philpott Lake, Rte. 6, Box 140, Bassett, VA 24055, or phone (703) 629-2703.

McLean

Colvin Run Mill Park (11 miles west of McLean, via VA 123, VA 7, on Colvin Run Road in Great Falls). The historic complex of this 18-acre park includes a restored miller's house, where works by artists and craftsmen are exhibited; a renovated barn with exhibits; and a 19th-century mill. An old-time general store sells flour products ground at the mill, handcrafted items, penny candy, and other goods.

Open daily 10 to 5, 12 to 5 Sunday. Closed Tuesdays, as well as January through mid-March, Christmas, and New Year's Day. Park grounds, Miller's House, Barn, and General Store all free. Guided tour through the mill on the hour and half-hour, first tour 10 A.M., last tour 4:30 P.M.; admission charge. Picnic area.

Dranesville Tavern (15 miles west of McLean via VA 7; or 11 miles west of Tysons Corner). Built in the early 1800s, this restored tavern was a rest stop for drovers who transported everything from flocks of geese to hogsheads of tobacco along the route now known as the Leesburg Turnpike. There is a guided tour through the authentically furnished boarding rooms and the kitchen.

Open Saturday and Sunday, 12 to 5. Closed during January and February, Thanksgiving, Christmas, and New Year's Day. Admission charge. Picnic area.

Evans Farm Inn (1696 Chain Bridge Rd., via VA 123). A day of sightseeing in the Sully Plantation, Woodlawn, and Mount Vernon areas would be nicely complemented by luncheon or dinner at Evans Farm Inn. Old farm equipment, hand-hewn timbers, antique furniture, fireplaces, and primitive cooking utensils create an inviting Early American decor. Lunches and dinners include such tempting selections as Roast Duckling with Spicy Prune and Orange Sauce, Martha Washington Cheese Cake, and Nellie Custis Caramel Custard.

A gift shop contains antiques, and there is a reconstructed log smokehouse adjacent to the inn, an old mill, and farm animals for children to feed.

Buffet luncheon daily except Sunday, 11:30 to 2:30. Dinners daily 5 to 9 P.M., Friday and Saturday 5 to 10 P.M., Sunday 11 to 9 P.M. Sunday brunch to 2 P.M. Closed Christmas Day. Reservations suggested, phone (703) 356-8000; no reservations accepted for Saturday evenings.

Claude Moore Colonial Farm (2 miles east of McLean on VA 193, Old Georgetown Pike). This small farm shows how a typical farm family would have lived in the late 1700s. Costumed attendants perform chores, raise crops, and tend to animals just as farmers did in the past.

Free; open Wednesday through Sunday, April through December. Closed Thanksgiving, Christmas, and rainy days.

Middleburg

Aldie Mill (5 miles east of Middleburg, on VA 50). This old mill, a Virginia Historic Landmark, was built in 1807 and contains its original pegged wooden beams, fireplace, and millstone hoist.

Red Fox Inn (Washington and Madison streets). Spend the night in the second oldest inn still in operation in America, built ca. 1728, in rooms with period furnishings and fireplaces. The quaint dining room specializes in continental cuisine.

Open year round for breakfast, lunch, and dinner. Dining and overnight reservations recommended; phone (703) 687-6301.

Valley View Vineyard (1 mile east of Middleburg on U.S. 50). Taste and buy quality wines, delicious foods, and selected crafts from their Virginia farm winery. A Wine Festival is held here annually, with demonstrations of how to taste and enjoy wines, cork-throwing and grape-stompin' contests, barrel-rolling races, and much much more.

For ticket information and a schedule of events, write Vinifera Wine Growers Association, P.O. Box P, The Plains, Virginia 22171, or phone (703) 754-8564. For a complete guide to Virginia vineyards and peach orchards, many where growers allow you to pick your own fruit, send a self-addressed, business-sized, stamped envelope to: Guides, VDACS/Division of Markets, P.O. Box 1163, Richmond, VA 23209.

Middletown

Belle Grove (1 1/4 miles south of Middletown on U.S. 11). This classical structure of hewn limestone was built in 1794 by Isaac Hite (brother-in-law of James Madison), and Thomas Jefferson contributed to its design. Union soldiers scratched their names on the attic walls during the Civil War when the house served as Federal headquarters for generals Fremont and Sheridan. More than 6,000 soldiers were killed in the October 19, 1864, Battle of Cedar Creek, fought on the adjacent farmland.

Today Belle Grove is a working plantation. A popular event here is Farm Craft Days, held during the annual July Wheat Harvest Festival, when visitors can see skilled craftsmen and women at work making patchwork quilts, forging horseshoes, square dancing to mountain music, and demonstrating other American crafts. Other annual events include traditional craft workshops, a needlework show, an oriental rug show, and an old-fashioned country Christmas celebration.

Open 10 to 4 Monday through Saturday, 1 to 5 Sunday, April through October. Admission charge.

Wayside Inn (on U.S. 11). This gracious inn has been lodging travelers since 1797. It was once a way station for stagecoach passengers, and during the Civil War it was used by soldiers of the North and South as they passed through the Shenandoah Valley region.

Each of the rooms has colonial furnishings, some with fireplaces and canopy beds. Dining-room attendants wear period costumes and serve dishes prepared from 200-year-old recipes.

Nearby is Wayside Wonderland, with facilities for swimming, picnicking, boating, and fishing.

Open year round. Three meals served daily (except Sundays and holidays, breakfast and dinner only). Reservations suggested; write Wayside Inn, U.S. Route 11, South, Middletown, VA 22645, or phone (703) 869-1797.

Wayside Theatre (on U.S. 11, I-81 exit 77). From July through Labor Day weekend, summer-stock plays are performed here.

Performances Wednesday through Sunday, June to September. For reservations, phone (703) 869-1776.

Monterey

The popular annual Highland Maple Festival is held here the last two weekends in March. There are demonstrations of sugar making, using antique sugar-making equipment, and tours of the sugar camps.

For more information, contact the Highland County Chamber of Commerce, P.O. Box 223, Monterey, VA 24465, or phone (703) 468-2550.

Maple Museum (south of Monterey on U.S. 220). The history of sugar making is exhibited here.

Open free daily.

Montross

Stratford Hall Plantation (6 miles north of Montross on VA 3 to Lerty, then east on VA 214). The entrance to Stratford Hall, one of the loveliest and most extensively developed of Virginia's historical plantations, is over the same road used 200 years ago by the famous Lee family. Two family members were signers of the Declaration of Independence, another introduced the motion for independence in the Continental Congress, and Robert E. Lee was general of the Armies of the Confederacy. The road now leads to a large, modern Visitor Center, which features an audiovisual program and a museum containing artifacts belonging to the Lee family, including Robert E. Lee's handwritten farewell orders to his Confederate forces.

The H-shaped house was built in the 1720s by Thomas Lee, planter, founder of the Ohio Company, and acting governor of Virginia. The 18 rooms, including 16 fireplaces, are authentically furnished with such rare pieces as Robert E. Lee's hand-carved crib, found in the "Mother's Room" where four generations of Lees were born; an unusual "horsehoof foot" table in the stately dining room; and a 17th-century clock with only an hour hand, sufficient for the needs of colonial America.

Oyster-shell paths in the garden lead to the furnished Coach House and Stable containing 18th- and 19th-century

Stratford Hall Plantation, near Fredericksburg

coaches. In the kitchen, with its huge fireplace large enough for several people to stand in, guests are greeted with home-made ginger cookies and apple cider.

A log-cabin dining room is located in a wooded setting on the plantation grounds and serves lunch from 11 to 3, April through October. Snacks are available year round. A trail leads to a spectacular cliff view of the Potomac River and a working mill where corn, barley, oats, and wheat are ground just as they were hundreds of years ago (mill grindings are sold at the Stratford Store).

Open daily 9 to 4:30; closed Christmas Day. Admission charge. Picnic area.

Westmoreland State Park (5 miles northwest of Montross on VA 3, then north on VA 347). This 1,302-acre park is situated on the Potomac River between Wakefield, George Washington's birthplace, and Stratford Hall, birthplace of Robert E. Lee. The area offers swimming, water-skiing, boat rentals and ramp, fishing, bicycling, and hiking on nature trails. A Visitor Center offers evening programs; cafe for dining; tent and trailer sites (April through November); cabins (May through September). Standard fees.

Mountain Lake

Mountain Lake Resort (west of Mountain Lake on VA 700, 7 miles north of VA 460). This resort hotel, high in the Allegheny Mountains, also has cottage accommodations. Recreational activities include swimming and boating, lawn games, recreation room, lighted tennis courts, horseback riding, movies, and dancing. Box lunches available.

Open June through September. For more information, phone (703) 626-7121.

Natural Bridge

Natural Bridge (on U.S. 11 and I-81, between exits 49 and 50, and 14 miles south of I-64). Natural Bridge is a great arch of grey limestone carved by the action of swirling water over millions of years. It rises 215 feet above Cedar Creek—55 feet higher than Niagara Falls. The Monocan Indians worshiped it and called it "The Bridge of God." George Washington surveyed the property and left his initials carved in stone, still visible today. Thomas Jefferson once owned the bridge, purchasing it from King George III of England for 20 shillings in 1774. During the Revolutionary War, American colonists let drops of molten lead fall from the top of the arch into the cold water below, turning the drops into bullets. The bridge was visited by John Marshall, Henry Clay, James Monroe, Daniel Boone, and Samuel Houston.

The bridge can be reached by bus or by a paved footpath bordered by a stream and thousand-year-old arborvitae trees. (Visitors may wish to take the bus back up, since the return walk is quite steep.) A 45-minute outdoor pageant, the *Drama of Creation,* is presented under the bridge nightly. The Bridge Entrance Building contains a cafeteria and snack bar; doors open at 7 A.M. for breakfast. To reserve overnight accommodations, write: Reservation Department, Box F, Natural Bridge, VA 24578, or phone (703) 291-2121.

Open 7 A.M. until dusk year round. Admission charge. Picnic area.

Natural Bridge Caverns (adjacent to Natural Bridge, on U.S. 11 and I-81, between exits 49 and 50, and 14 miles south of I-64). These caverns offer visitors the unique experience of seeing an underground canyon 34 stories beneath the earth's surface. The one-hour guided tour winds past colossal limestone formations and pools of water, then returns to the Visitor Center.

Open daily March through November; closed December, January, and February. Times vary with the seasons. Admission charge. Picnic area.

Natural Bridge Wax Museum and Factory Tour (on Natural Bridge Parking Lot, on U.S. 11 and I-81, between exits 49 and 50, and 14 miles south of I-64). Shenandoah Valley history is the focus of the exhibits in this wax museum, with more than 125 life-sized replicas of historical figures in natural settings. Today's visitors to Natural Bridge will be particularly interested in seeing how that attraction was reached in the 1800s. A wax exhibit depicts those hearty souls being raised in the air in a small iron cage operated by a hand-cranked winch, which then lowered them into the gorge below. After your visit to the museum, you will be taken on a guided factory tour, where you will see the amazing process of how wax figures are made.

Open daily March to November. Admission charge. Picnic area.

Natural Bridge Zoo (exit 50S or 49 off I-81, 1 mile north of Natural Bridge on U.S. 11). This baby-animal zoo houses gentle fawns, llamas, lambs, and other species for youngsters to hold, pet, and feed.

Open 9 to 6, April through November. Admission charge. Picnic area.

New Market

Endless Caverns (exit 66 or 67 off I-81, north of New Market). Discovered in 1879 by two boys chasing a rabbit across a field, the caverns received their name when explorations failed to find an end to the winding passageways. Truly spectacular displays of the wonders of nature await the visitor in these caverns, whose chambers have yet to be completely explored. The guided tour lasts approximately one hour, 15 minutes.

Open 9 to 9 June 11 through Labor Day, 9 to 5 the rest of the year. Closed Christmas Day. Admission charge. Areas for picnicking and camping, and a lake for swimming, boating, and fishing. For campground information and reservations, write: Endless Caverns, P.O. Box 859, New Market, VA 22844, or phone (703) 740-3993.

New Market Battlefield Park (1 1/2 miles north of New Market, exit 67 off I-81, on VA 305). One of the most heroic episodes of the Civil War occurred here on May 15, 1864, when 247 Virginia Military Institute cadets, mostly teenagers without battle experience, fought in the front lines against veteran Union troops in the Battle of New Market. Outnumbered by an advancing Union army led by Gen. Franz Sigel, Confederate general John C. Breckinridge desperately ordered the young cadets at V.M.I.—90 miles away in Lexington—into service. The cadets were supposed to be kept in reserve, but when they arrived after a forced march of three days, they joined the fighting in the front lines. They captured a battery, and their fighting spirit helped drive back the Union forces and turn the tide of battle.

Of the 57 youths wounded, 10 died. Their names have been inscribed in the 28-foot stained-glass window dedicated to the V.M.I. cadets in the Visitor's Center at the park. A panoramic survey of the Civil War is presented in the circular, two-story Virginia Room through murals, dioramas, photographs, three-dimensional figures, and recordings. An award-winning 12-minute film tells the cadets' story, and a 16-minute film depicts Stonewall Jackson's 1862 Shenandoah Valley Campaign.

Free maps are provided to guide the visitors on a one-mile walking tour of battle lines, the restored and furnished Bushong Farmhouse (open daily 10 to 4:30, mid-June to Labor Day), the Wheelwright House, outbuildings, and replicas of

Union cannon. Each year on the second Sunday in May the Battle of New Market is reenacted for thousands.

Open daily 9 to 5. Closed Christmas Day. Admission charge.

Shenandoah Caverns (four miles north of New Market, exit 68 off I-81). The unusual rock formations of these caverns (their "bacon" formations were pictured in *National Geographic*) are conveniently reached by elevators. They descend more than 200 feet beneath the earth's surface and open into the vast, subterranean chambers of the cave. Tours every 20 minutes.

Open daily, closed Christmas. Admission charge. Picnic area, coffee shop, antique shop.

Tuttle and Spice General Store and Free Village Museum (exit 68 off I-81). These offer the visitor such old-fashioned delicacies as Amish Maid Fudge, more than 80 kinds of other candies, Virginia hams and bacon, sandwiches and snacks, plus a collection of leather jewelry, tinware, and more. A village of seven old shops along gaslit streets provides pleasant browsing down memory lane.

Open free daily. Closed Thanksgiving, Christmas, and New Year's Day.

Newport News

This city is the site of the world's largest shipbuilding company, the Newport News Shipbuilding and Dry Dock Company. With two other cities—Norfolk and Portsmouth—it makes up the Port of Hampton Roads, 14 miles long and 40 feet deep, and one of the finest natural harbors in the world. Shipbuilding has been an industry in Newport News since 1886. It was here that the construction was done for the U.S. aircraft carrier *Enterprise,* the world's first nuclear-powered ship, and the U.S. aircraft carrier the *John F. Kennedy.*

In the historical records of the Virginia Company in 1619, "Newportes Newes" appears as the name of one of the earliest colonial settlements. The town was named after Capt. Christopher Newport, commander of the ships that brought the first settlers to Jamestown, who brought the "news" to the settlers along with their supplies. The site is listed on Capt. John Smith's map of Virginia, drawn in 1608, as "Point Hope," named during an early landing here.

Beginning at the intersection of VA 17 and VA 143, gold and blue signs mark points of interest along a self-guided auto tour. For further information, write: Newport News Department of Recreation, Parks and Public Relations, City Hall, Newport News, VA 23607, or the Virginia Peninsula Tourism and Conference Bureau, Patrick Henry International Airport, Newport News, VA 23602, or phone (804) 881-9777.

Army Transportation Museum at Fort Eustis (northwest of Newport News, off I-64, Ft. Eustis exit). This museum depicts the history of Army military transportation, beginning with the Revolutionary War. A collection of military vehicles is on display on the grounds outside.

Free, open 8 to 5 Monday through Friday; 10 to 5 Saturday and holidays; 12 to 5 Sunday. Closed Christmas and New Year's Day.

Mariners Museum (at intersection of U.S. 60, Warwick Boulevard, and VA 312, J. Clyde Morris Boulevard). This depository of one of the world's largest nautical collections was founded in 1930 by Archer M. Huntington, son of Newport News Shipyard founder Collis P. Huntington. The park entrance is marked with the 17-foot-diameter, golden propeller from the battleship *South Dakota*. Inside the Great Hall of the museum, a 1 1/2-ton gilded eagle figurehead soars above on walls lined with marine memorabilia. Spacious galleries contain ships' models, carvings, photographs, costumes, tools, weapons, the Crabtree collection of carved miniature ship models, relics devoted to the whaling industry, and decorative porcelain, glass, china, brass, and silver. A research library contains photographs, rare books, and maps pertaining to the sea. In an adjoining courtyard, visitors can inspect an old steam tug's pilothouse and see a collection of small craft from around the world, from dugout canoes to Chinese sampans.

A 550-acre wooded park surrounds the museum, with areas designated for boating, freshwater fishing, bicycling, picnicking, and hiking.

Open 9 to 5, Monday through Saturday, 12 to 5 Sunday. Closed Christmas Day. Free admission to the park; admission charge to the museum. Boat rentals Friday through Sunday, daily in summer.

Newport News Park (1 mile north of junction of VA 105 and 143). This park offers something for every member of the family: nature trails; bicycle paths and rentals; archery; picnicking; lake fishing; boat rentals, canoes and paddleboats; arboretum; two 18-hole golf courses; nearly 200 campsites; and a museum.

Open daily; free. Tourist Information Center.

Virginia Living Museum (524 J. Clyde Morris Blvd.). The large, modern building housing this nature and science center and its surrounding wooded area offer an aquarium, planetarium, observatory with a 14-inch Celestron telescope, natural history exhibits, and nature trails. Special nature programs are held on Saturdays and Sundays.

Open 9 to 5 Monday through Saturday; 1 to 5 Sundays. Open 7 P.M. to 9 P.M. Thursdays. Closed Thanksgiving, December 24 and 25, and New Year's Day. Planetarium open daily July and August; Thursdays, Saturdays, and Sundays rest of year. Admission charge. For more information, phone (804) 595-1900.

War Memorial Museum of Virginia (9285 Warwick Blvd., U.S. 60). Four military tanks mark the entrance to this museum, with more than 18,000 exhibits and displays representing every conflict involving America, from pre-Revolutionary times to the Viet Nam War. There are military weapons, medals, grim reminders of World War II's Dachau prison camp, a collection of German helmets and military uniforms spanning two centuries, and the world's largest collection of wartime posters. A propeller from a captured World War II Japanese airplane was presented to the museum by Adm. Chester W. Nimitz.

Open 9 to 5 Monday through Saturday, 1 to 5 Sunday. Closed Thanksgiving, Christmas, and New Year's Day. Admission charge. Picnic area.

Wharton's Wharf Harbor Cruise. These narrated harbor cruises include views such as the Norfolk Naval Base, the coal piers of the C&O Railway, and the Newport News Shipyard. Trips offered are sightseeing cruises (2 hours), twilight cruises (2 1/2 hours), moonlight buffet cruises (4 hours), Sunday cruises to Waterside (5 hours), and Intracoastal Waterway and Jamestown Island cruises (8 hours).

Sailings daily April through October. For a schedule and fees, phone (804) 245-1533 or 877-6114.

Norfolk

Norfolk was founded by decree of King Charles II in 1682, when the General Assembly of Virginia, needing an ocean port, purchased the site from a settler for 10,000 pounds of tobacco. By the mid-1700s, Norfolk was a major seaport and the largest city in the state of Virginia. In 1753 the governor of Virginia presented Norfolk with a mace of silver, now kept in the vaults of the Virginia National Bank. A replica is on view in the historic Willoughby-Baylor House. During the Revolutionary War, the city was shelled by British troops under the command of Lord Dunmore. Later it was burned by American colonists to prevent its capture. The only building left unscathed by the fire and shelling was St. Paul's Church, where many of the townspeople had taken refuge.

Although it is one of America's oldest cities, Norfolk is also a modern metropolis with year-round resort activities. It was chosen as the headquarters for the Atlantic Fleet because of its superior harbor, Hampton Roads, the world's largest. Three four-year colleges are located here—Old Dominion University, Virginia Wesleyan College, and Norfolk State College.

The Chesapeake Bay Bridge-Tunnel (17 miles long) connects the city with the Eastern Shore, saving 95 miles and 1 1/2 hours of driving time between Norfolk-Virginia Beach and points north of the Delaware Memorial Bridge. Three miles out at sea, there is a stopover with restaurant, gift shop, and fishing pier (bait and tackle available). Car toll, including all passengers, $9.

For more information contact the Norfolk Visitors Bureau, 236 E. Plume St., Norfolk, VA 23510, or phone (804) 441-5266.

Chrysler Museum (Olney Road at Mowbray Arch). A multimillion-dollar art collection here has representative works from nearly every period of art history, including paintings by such masters as Van Dyck, El Greco, Rembrandt, Renoir, Rubens, Picasso, and Dali. The museum boasts the country's largest private collection of glassware.

Free; open daily 10 to 4 Tuesday through Saturday, 1 to 5 Sunday. Closed. Fourth of July, Thanksgiving, Christmas, and New Year's Day.

d'Art Center (Boush Street and Waterside Drive). Artists at work make and sell their paintings, photographs, sculpture, jewelry, and quilts.

Open free daily. Closed Thanksgiving, Christmas, and New Year's Day.

Hermitage Foundation Museum (7637 N. Shore Rd., near intersection of Hampton Boulevard, VA 337, and Little Creek Road, VA 165). This English Tudor mansion, an architectural masterpiece, was begun in 1906 by William and Florence K. Sloane and was in the making for 30 years. The 42 rooms are appointed with priceless art including oriental rugs, Chinese bronzes and jade, tapestries, antique furniture, and artwork from eight countries. During the guided tour, hostesses reveal storage compartments and passages to rooms hidden behind the rich carved oak and teak paneling. Located on the Lafayette River, about 12 acres of beautifully landscaped grounds are open free to the public during museum hours.

Open daily 10 to 5, 1 to 5 Sunday. Closed Thanksgiving, Christmas, and New Year's Day. Admission charge.

General Douglas MacArthur Memorial (City Hall Avenue and Bank Street). Although Douglas MacArthur was born in Fort Little Rock, Arkansas, he always considered Norfolk, his mother's birthplace, to be his home. The old City Hall, built in 1852, was dedicated as a museum in honor of General MacArthur, who lies buried within the Memorial Rotunda. MacArthur graduated first in his class at West Point and became the youngest general in World War I at the age of 38, the youngest man ever to become Army chief of staff, first United Nations Commander, and the winner of the Congressional Medal of Honor (the first time in the country's history that both a father and son received the honor). He was decorated 13 times, and his titles include Supreme Commander of the Allied Powers in Japan, Commander-in-Chief of the Far East, and Commander-in-Chief of the United Nations Command in Korea.

The memorial contains nine galleries of exhibits, including his famous corncob pipe, "scrambled eggs" cap, and sunglasses. Medals and honors awarded to him both here and abroad fill several cases, and there are valuable gifts of china and silver that were presented to him by the grateful people of the Philippines and Japan, whose nation he reconstructed under democratic guidelines after World War II. His 1950 Chrysler limousine, used when he was Supreme Commander in Japan, is on display next to the authentically furnished replica of his office in the Old State Department Building in Washington, D.C. Also here are exhibits of captured military weapons, the original, handwritten manuscript of his *Memoirs,* and two of the pens used to sign the surrender document aboard the U.S.S. *Missouri* on September 2, 1945, ending World War II.

An excellent 22-minute film about the General's life is shown continuously in an adjacent auditorium.

Free, open 10 to 5 Monday through Saturday, 11 to 5 Sunday. Closed Thanksgiving, Christmas, and New Year's Day. Gift shop and library.

Myers House (Freemason and Bank streets). Moses Myers, millionaire import-export magnate of 18th-century Norfolk, built this elegant, 1792 Georgian town house. Most of its original, luxurious furnishings still fill the rooms, including family portraits by Thomas Sully and Gilbert Stuart, who painted the picture of George Washington that appears on our dollar bill. The Dining Room often hosted such prominent guests as President James Monroe, Daniel Webster, and the Marquis De Lafayette. In the small Withdrawing Room are two chairs given to the Myers family by President Madison. The exquisite parlor fireplace has been reproduced and placed on display in the New York Metropolitan Museum.

Open 10 to 5 Tuesday through Saturday, 12 to 5 Sunday, April through December; 12 to 5 Tuesday through Saturday, January through March. Closed Mondays, Fourth of July, Thanksgiving, Christmas, and New Year's Day. Admission charge.

Norfolk Botanical Gardens, Gardens by the Sea (follow signs on Airport Road; gardens adjacent to Municipal Airport). The world's largest collection of azaleas and camellias is arrayed in these lush gardens, the site of Norfolk's International Azalea Festival each April. Tulips, crocus, iris, dogwood, and thousands of exotic plants and shrubs bloom along the lakes here throughout the season. Visitors can stroll along fragrant paths or take 30-minute narrated rides aboard trackless trains or along waterways on canal boats.

Open daily 8:30 to sunset. Admission charge. Train and canal boat tours daily mid-March through Labor Day; through October weekends, trains only. Restaurant, picnic area. Information Center (closed Christmas and New Year's Day).

Norfolk Naval Station and Norfolk Naval Air Station (Hampton and Admiral Taussig boulevards). This is the largest naval installation in the world. The bus tour of the base includes the Naval Supply Center, the overhaul and repair facilities for the Atlantic's Naval Air Force, modern submarines and ships, and supersonic jet fighters.

"Open House Ships" 1 to 4:30 Saturday and Sunday. Tour buses leave from Naval Tours and Information Office, 9808 Hampton Blvd. Half-hour tours daily April through October. Hampton Roads Naval Museum open daily.

Norfolk-Portsmouth Harbor Tours (end of West Main Street at Boush Street). Sail along the same route that Capt.

Christopher Newport and Capt. John Smith took to establish the first permanent English-speaking colony in the New World. Cruise over the battle areas of the *Monitor* and the *Merrimac*. See nuclear submarines, guided missile ships, destroyers, giant oil tankers, luxury liners, and the graveyard of ships. Tours are narrated 1 1/2- and 3-hour cruises aboard a replica of a 19th-century riverboat. Daytime and sunset cruises.

Tours daily. Schedule changes yearly; for information write Harbor Tours, end of Bay Street, Portsmouth, VA 23704, or phone (804) 393-4735.

Norfolk School of Boatbuilding (waterfront). Visitors may view boats under construction at this school for traditional maritime skills.

Open free Monday through Friday. Closed major holidays.

St. Paul's Episcopal Church (Saint Paul Boulevard and City Hall Avenue). During the British bombardment and burning of Norfolk in 1776, many frightened colonial townspeople took refuge in this church, the only structure that survived the holocaust. A stray cannonball fired from a British warship hit the walls, where it is still embedded. The small cemetery surrounding the 1739 church contains graves dating back to 1673, and a museum houses exhibits relating to the church's history.

Open, free, 10 A.M. to 4:30 P.M. Tuesday through Saturday; 2 to 4:30 P.M. Sunday. No tours on holidays; closed Mondays, Memorial Day, Independence Day, Christmas, New Year's, and Labor Day.

Virginia Zoological Park (3500 Granby St.). A zoo and conservatory, playground, basketball and tennis courts, boat ramp, and picnic area are contained in this 55-acre park.

Open 10 to 5 daily. Closed Christmas and New Year's Day. Admission charge, except free 10 to 11 A.M. daily.

The Waterside (333 Waterside Dr.). This waterfront pavilion features more than 120 shops, bazaars, restaurants, open-air food stands, and live entertainment. Adjacent is Town Point Park, where harbor cruises depart several times a day. The cruise ship *New Spirit* offers evening dinner and moonlight party cruises, with buffet dining, dancing, and entertainment. For reservations phone (804) 627-7771. A short ride on a paddle-wheeler at the docks of Waterside takes the visitor to the open-air shops of Portsmouth.

Open free daily.

Willoughby-Baylor House (E. Freemason and Cumberland streets). This charming 1794 house is a good example of an upper-middle-class dwelling in 18th-century Norfolk. One room is filled with historic relics, such as the ship's bell from the U.S.S. *Merrimac* and part of the Confederate flag cut down from Lee's headquarters following his surrender at Appomattox Court House in 1865. The remainder of the house contains 18th-century furnishings. Of special interest are President Madison's dining table from the White House, a 1710 wall mirror made with divided glass (to escape paying the tax on large glass mirrors), and a rare 1697 British sixpence, found in one of the chairs when it was sent out to be reupholstered.

Open 10 to 5 Tuesday through Saturday, 12 to 5 Sunday, April through December; 12 to 5 Tuesday through Saturday, January through March. Closed Mondays and Fourth of July, Thanksgiving, Christmas, and New Year's Day. Admission charge.

Orange

Orange County on U.S. 15 was the home of James Madison, the fourth president of the United States. He and his wife, Dolley, spent their retirement years here at Montpelier. The Madison Graveyard (six miles west of Orange, one mile off VA 20) is open to visitors and contains the remains of both Madison and Dolley.

Zachary Taylor, the 12th president of the United States and a cousin of Madison's, was born in Orange. A meeting between Madison and a Baptist preacher resulted in the religious freedom clause in our Bill of Rights. The event is commemorated by a stone marker and bronze tablet in Leland Memorial Park, six miles east of Orange on Route 20.

James Madison Museum (129 Caroline St.). Historical relics and exhibits depict Madison's youth and education, his participation in the Revolution, his presidency in 1809, and "Mr. Madison's War," the War of 1812.

Open 9 to 5 Monday through Friday, 12 to 4 Saturday and Sunday, March through November; Monday through Friday only December through February. Admission charge. Closed Thanksgiving, Christmas, and New Year's Day.

Montpelier (4 miles west of Orange, one mile off VA 20). There are guided tours of James and Dolley Madison's mansion and a shuttle bus tour of the grounds.

Open daily. Closed Thanksgiving, Christmas, and New Year's Day. Admission charge.

Ordinary

Seawall's Ordinary (on Route 17, 5 miles north of the York River Bridge, near Yorktown). Seawall's Ordinary offers a tempting variety of native and international cuisine. George Washington stopped here whenever he visited his grandparents at Warner Hall, and Lafayette dined here while the French fleet was anchored in the York River. In colonial days, an "Ordinary" was a resting place where a traveler could get a meal or a beverage and have his horses fed. Today, visitors can enjoy the same Southern hospitality in this completely renovated 1757 structure, which offers dining by a fireplace in winters, or on a patio in summers, weather permitting.

Reservations suggested; phone (804) 642-3635.

Petersburg

This city began as a small trading post and fort in 1645 and quickly grew into an important tobacco and transportation center. Cornwallis assembled his troops here on his way to Yorktown, and during the Civil War the city endured a ten-month siege by the Union army.

The Visitor Center offers free brochures for the self-guided tour. For more information, write: Petersburg Visitor

Center, 19 Bollingbrook St., P.O. Box 2107, Petersburg, VA 23804, or phone (804) 733-2400. The Center is located in the 19th-century Farmers Bank (see below).

Open 9 to 5 daily, closed Thanksgiving, December 24 and 25, and New Year's Day. Free.

Farmers Bank (19 Bollingbrook St.). One of the oldest bank buildings in the United States, Farmers Bank failed in 1865 after investing most of its resources in Confederate bonds. It has been restored to its former appearance and furnished with banking relics from the 19th century, including the bank's old printing press and plates and huge strongbox. Visitors can sit inside the double bank vault and watch an audiovisual program on the history of early American banking. The bank also serves as home to the Petersburg Visitor Center.

Free; open daily 9 to 5, Monday through Saturday; 1 to 5 Sunday. Closed Thanksgiving, December 24 and 25, and New Year's Day.

Old Blandford Church and Cemetery (on VA routes 301 and 460 on Crater Road). Blandford Church was erected in 1735 to serve Bristol Parish of the Church of England; it became a memorial chapel and Confederate shrine in 1901. Thirteen Confederate states donated Tiffany windows to the church, with the Ladies Memorial Association sponsoring the 14th, and Tiffany himself presenting the 15th. It is the only building in the United States where every window is a Tiffany. To be seen at its greatest beauty, the church should be viewed just before sunset, when the falling rays of light strike the stained glass.

A Church Interpretation Center has an audiovisual program and free maps showing the cemetery's points of interest. Monuments and gravestones—including 30,000 Confederate graves—commemorate soldiers of every conflict in which Americans have fought. Captain McRae, who fought in the War of 1812, is buried here, and William Phillips, the only British general to lie in American soil, was secretly buried by his men somewhere behind the church. There are also a number of gravestones of early colonists, chiefly from Scotland, England, and Ireland. The oldest tombstone dates back to 1702, before the church itself was built.

Free; open daily 9 to 5 Monday through Saturday, 12 to 5 Sunday. Closed Thanksgiving, December 24 and 25, and New Year's Day.

Poplar Grove National Cemetery (3 miles south of Petersburg on VA 675). Part of the self-guided tour of Petersburg National Battlefield, this cemetery contains the graves of more than 6,000 Civil War casualties. More than 4,000 of the graves are unidentified.

Quartermaster Museum (3 miles northeast of Petersburg at Fort Lee on VA 36). U.S. Army Quartermaster Corps displays here date from 1775, with 25 tour areas ranging from historical uniforms to equestrian equipment. Flags, featured throughout the museum, include American flags from 1659 to the present, presidential banners, and the original 50-star flag presented to President Eisenhower. The Memorial Room contains relics from the World War II aircraft *Lady Be Good,* lost over the Libyan Desert in 1943 and not discovered until 16 years later. John J. Pershing's office furniture shares space with George S. Patton's jeep—complete with air horns on the hood—used to herald his entry into areas captured by Third Army forces in 1944. A display of rations dates back to the Revolutionary War. The thousands of insignias and decorations include the revered Medal of Honor; weapons, musical instruments, and even dog equipment are just a few of the other collections. Free maps aid the visitor on the self-guided tour.

Open, free, 8 to 5 Monday through Friday, 11 to 5 Saturday, Sunday, and holidays. Closed Thanksgiving, Christmas, and New Year's Day. Gift shop.

Saint Paul's Episcopal Church (110 N. Union St., between Tabb and W. Washington streets). Gen. Robert E. Lee and other Confederate leaders worshiped here. The pew that Lee occupied is marked.

Open 9 to 1 Monday through Friday, June through August; 8:30 to 3 September through May. (Go to the Parish House door, to the left, for admittance.)

Siege Museum (15 W. Bank St.). Scenes of the ten-month siege of Petersburg during the Civil War are displayed in this museum.

Open, free, 9 to 5 Monday through Saturday, 1 to 5 Sunday. Closed Thanksgiving, December 24 and 25, and New Year's Day. Film shown on the hour every hour.

Petersburg National Battlefield

In the longest siege in the history of American warfare, generals Robert E. Lee and Ulysses S. Grant waged a fierce ten-month trench battle here during 1864 and 1865. Losses totaled more than 70,000 men, with infection and disease accounting for the greatest number of deaths.

Grant's campaign to capture the Confederate capital at Richmond began in early May 1864, with the battles of the Wilderness west of Fredericksburg. Failing to break through Lee's lines in frontal assaults, Grant swung his forces behind Petersburg and attempted to cut off Lee's railroad supply lines. Lee moved his army of 50,000 men down from Richmond, and for four days held a defense line against Grant's 112,000 attacking forces. In mid-June, Grant gave orders to lay siege to the city. Both sides had already built many fortifications, and eventually the earth forts and trenches formed a great arch stretching around the city for nearly 40 miles, the largest single battlefield in the United States. The end of the struggle came on April 1, 1865, when Gen. Philip H. Sheridan swept through Five Forks, 17 miles southwest of Petersburg, cutting Lee's last railroad supply line and forcing him to abandon his defense of Richmond. Appomattox— and the final surrender—was but a week away.

At the Visitor Center, displays, dioramas, and photographs show the ingenious engineering of the siege fortifications. A seating area around a circular map screen allows visitors to watch changing battlelines while listening to a 17-minute recorded talk (given hourly) on the history of the siege.

Points of interest along the battlefield tour are earthwork fortifications, gun emplacements, forts, and the original "Dictator," a 17,000-pound Union mortar requiring 14 pounds of powder to fire a 200-pound explosive shell into Petersburg, 2 1/2 miles away.

The self-guided tour also includes the site of the Crater, the remains of a huge tunnel secretly built by coal miners in the Federal army beneath the Confederate fortifications along the siege lines. Union troops set off four tons of gunpowder in the tunnel on July 30, 1864, killing the entire 300-man garrison in the fort above and leaving a gaping hole 170 feet long, 60 feet wide, and 30 feet deep. Union forces easily occupied the crater, but became trapped inside the high walls. While thousands of men milled blindly around inside, the Confederates returned and began to fire down into the massed troops. When the fighting was over, 4,000 Union soldiers and 1,500 Confederates lay dead.

The battlefield is located off VA 36, east of Petersburg. Visitor Center open, free, 8 A.M. to 7 P.M. Memorial Day through Labor Day, 8 to 5 the rest of the year. Closed Christmas and New Year's Day. Park open, free, 8 A.M. till dusk year round. Living history programs, with demonstrations of the use of cannon, mortar, and small arms, are presented from the middle of June through Labor Day. Picnic area.

Portsmouth

Capt. John Smith explored the site of this city in 1608, and a grant for settlement was issued 12 years later. The excellent deepwater harbor facilities here quickly developed Portsmouth into one of the country's major shipbuilding centers, in business since 1767. The world's first ironclad vessel, the *Merrimac*, was built at this shipyard by the Confederates in 1861.

The Trinity Church (Episcopal, 500 Court St.) dates back to 1762, and the Monumental United Church (Queen and Dinwiddle streets) of 1772 is the oldest Methodist church in the South. Many historic homes, some dating back to the early colonial period, may be viewed.

Information on the self-guided tour is available at the Portsmouth Chamber of Commerce, 524 Middle St., phone (804) 397-3453.

Norfolk-Portsmouth Harbor Tours (end of High Street). See listing under *Norfolk* for details.

Portsmouth Lightship Museum (London Slip and Water Street). Housed aboard a former Coast Guard ship, this floating museum has all types of Coast Guard relics on display. The quarters of the crew and commanding officer are authentically furnished, and the radio gear and other equipment are operative. Across the parking lot is the Portsmouth Naval Shipyard Museum.

Open, free, 10 to 5 Tuesday through Saturday, 1 to 5 Sunday and Thanksgiving Day. Closed Mondays, Christmas, and New Year's Day.

Portsmouth Naval Shipyard Museum (2 High St.). Portsmouth naval history is the focus here, with weaponry dating from colonial muskets to modern missiles. Displays include flags, uniforms, ship models, and naval equipment.

Free; open 10 to 5 Tuesday through Saturday, 1 to 5 Sunday. Closed Mondays, Thanksgiving, Christmas, and New Year's Day.

Quantico

U.S. Marine Corps Air-Ground Museum (on Marine Corps Base, off I-95). There are two aviation museums here, one featuring the development of aviation from 1912 to 1940, and the other focusing on the World War II years, from 1941 to 1945. The Hall of Heroes is devoted to famous marine aviators; some of the collections include displays of weaponry, U.S. and Japanese uniforms, and authentic aircraft.

Open 10 to 4 Tuesday through Friday; 10 to 5 Saturday, Sunday, and holidays, April through late November. Closed Mondays. Visitor passes and directions available at the main gate. Free.

Radford

Now a modern city and the home of Radford University (on U.S. 11, exit 35 off I-81) and Claytor Lake State Park (on VA 660, 6 miles southwest of Radford, exit 33 off I-81), this area was once the hunting ground of the Shawnee and Cherokee Indian tribes and the site of many massacres. In 1755 Mary Draper Ingles was captured by Indians on land that is now part of Blacksburg and forced on an arduous journey over 800 miles away to Ohio. Somehow she escaped and made her way back home to her husband. They moved and settled in Radford, where the outdoor drama of her experience, *The Long Way Home,* is performed at the site of their log cabin.

For more information, contact the Chamber of Commerce, 1126 Norwood St., Radford, VA 24141, or phone (703) 639-2202.

Claytor Lake State Park (6 miles southwest of Radford, on VA 660, south of I-81 exit 33). A 5,000-acre lake and 472-acre wooded park provide swimming, water-skiing, fishing, boating (marina and ramp), horseback riding, hiking, and picnicking facilities. Cabins are available May through September. Tent and camping sites open April through November. Concession and Visitor Center. Admission charge.

The Long Way Home. For reservations and information, write: *The Long Way Home,* Box 711, Radford, VA 24141, or phone (703) 639-0679. Performances 8:30 P.M., Thursday through Sunday, mid-June through late August; nightly 8:30 P.M. August 21 through August 30.

Richmond

On May 23, 1607, just ten days after they landed at Jamestown to establish the first permanent English settlement, captains John Smith and Christopher Newport sailed to the falls of the James River, the future site of Richmond. A frontier fort was built here in 1644, and a settlement was established in 1742. By 1779 the city had so grown in importance that it replaced Williamsburg as the state capital.

Richmond also served as the capital of the Confederacy during the four years of the Civil War, with Federal armies launching drive after drive to capture it. After the grueling ten-month-long siege of Petersburg (see *Petersburg National*

Battlefield), Lee's troops were finally forced to abandon Richmond's defense. Her own citizens burned the city to keep it from falling into enemy hands, evacuating it in April of 1865.

Four kinds of tours are available: group tours, individualized tours with guides, walking tours about the town, and auto tours with recorded tapes. Trips include visits to such historic sites as the State Capitol Building, a Tudor mansion built in the 15th century, and historic Saint John's Church, 35 years older than America itself, where Patrick Henry made his famous "Give me liberty or give me death" speech. Plantation tours include the Richmond-Petersburg-Williamsburg areas. For information contact the Metro Richmond Visitor Center, 1700 Robin Hood Rd., Richmond, VA 23220, or phone (804) 358-5511. There are four colleges and universities: Virginia Commonwealth University at 828 W. Franklin St., Virginia Union University at 1500 N. Lombardy St., Union Theological Seminary at 3401 Brook Rd., and the University of Richmond. Information is available at the Convention and Visitors Bureau, 300 E. Main St., Richmond, VA 23219, or phone (804) 782-2777 or 358-5511.

Agecroft Hall (4305 Sulgrave Rd., 1/2 mile off VA 147, Cary Street, in Windsor Farms). Step back into a different century in a different country and discover how an English gentleman would have lived when Henry VII was King of England. This Tudor residence—once part of a much larger estate and surrounded by a protective moat—was built about 1480 near Manchester, England. The land where it stood was inherited in 1374 by Roger de Langley, a member of a family that had come to England with William the Conqueror. Through the centuries little change was made to the original structure except for minor additions. By the 1900s, however, the estate had fallen into ruin and was in danger of collapsing from having been undercut by a coal mine. In 1925, Thomas C. Williams, Jr., of Richmond, purchased Agecroft Hall and had it disassembled brick by brick for shipment to Richmond, where it was reconstructed on a site overlooking the James River. To create an English countryside setting, elaborate formal gardens of boxwood hedges, flower beds, sparkling fountains, and grassy meadows were placed around the estate.

The tour of Agecroft Hall begins with an audiovisual program of its history, followed by a guided tour. Rooms are furnished with authentic period pieces, including old tapestries, hand-carved furniture, and metal suits of armor. King Charles I of England attended a wedding in this house; he left the name of the bridegroom and the date—July 12, 1645—scratched in a windowpane where it is still visible today.

Open daily 10 to 4 Tuesday through Friday, 2 to 5 Saturday and Sunday. Closed Mondays and holidays. Nominal admission charge. Next door is another authentic Tudor residence, the Virginia House; a few blocks away is the Wilton House, built in 1750.

Bryan Park (Bellevue Avenue and Hermitage Road). This park is best distinguished for its late April to mid-May display of azaleas. Tennis courts, picnic area.

Admission charge for vehicles, weekends and holidays.

City Hall Observation Deck (Ninth and Broad streets). Visitors can get a sweeping view of the city from the 18th floor here.

Open free Monday through Friday.

Half Way House (10301 Jefferson Davis Highway, exit 6A off I-95). No attempt has been made to disguise the age of this small 1760 inn that once served as the rest stop and horse-change station for the Petersburg Coach. Among its famous guests were Washington, Patrick Henry, Lafayette, Lee, and Grant. Now visitors may enjoy the exceptional food and service that have earned this historic inn a national reputation.

Lunch 11:30 to 2:30 Sunday through Friday (lunch not served Saturdays). Dinner 5:30 to 9:30 Sunday through Thursday, 5:30 to 10 Friday and Saturday. For reservations phone (804) 275-1760. No overnight facilities.

Hollywood Cemetery (Cherry and Albemarle streets). This 1847 cemetery contains the graves of Confederate President Jefferson Davis and his family, Confederate generals J.

E. B. Stuart and Fitzhugh Lee, U.S. presidents Monroe and Tyler, and thousands of Confederates killed in the Civil War.

Free; open 7:30 A.M. to 6 P.M. Monday through Saturday, April through September; to 5 P.M. October through March; open 8 A.M. on Sundays. Audiovisual program, Monday through Friday.

James River Park. Whitewater canoe and inner tube accesses down the James River, next to a major metropolitan area, are available here, with other areas open to fishing, bicycling, and hiking.

Open free daily. Visitor Center.

James River and Kanawha Canal Locks (12th and Byrd streets). Dating back to George Washington's time, these canal locks carried vessels around the falls of the James River. An audiovisual program explains the history of the canal.

Open, free, 9 to 5 daily.

Robert E. Lee House (707 E. Franklin St.). General Lee lived here from 1864 to 1865 and returned after the surrender of his Confederate forces at Appomattox. The restored house contains furnishings that once belonged to the Lee family.

John Marshall House (818 E. Marshall St.). Designed by the distinguished Chief Justice himself, and built in the late 1700s, this was the home of John Marshall until he died in 1835. Our nation's Liberty Bell received its famous crack when it was tolled at his death. Many original furnishings are on display.

Open Tuesday through Sunday. Closed most major holidays and Mondays. Admission charge.

Maymont Park (Pennsylvania Avenue and Hampton Street). This unusual park has Japanese and Italian gardens to stroll in, an aviary and wildlife exhibit, an art collection housed in the Dooley Mansion, and a children's farm.

Park entrance free; open daily, 10 to 7 April through October, 10 to 5 November through March.

Meadow Farm Museum (12 miles northwest of Richmond on I-95N, I-295W, exit Woodman Road S., at Courtney and Mountain roads). Farm life in the mid-1800s is depicted here. Surrounding the farmhouse are a barn, outbuildings, farm animals, vegetable gardens, and orchards.

Open Tuesday through Sunday. Closed Mondays and the months of January and February. Admission charge.

Monument Avenue (west of the downtown area from Lombardy Street). Restored town houses face across this hand-paved boulevard, lined with equestrian statues of Confederate generals Stuart, Lee, and Jackson; of Jefferson Davis; and of Commodore Matthew Fontaine Maury. Commodore Maury invented the electric torpedo for Confederate coastal defense.

Museum and White House of the Confederacy (1201 E. Clay St.). This building once served as the White House of the Confederacy; Confederate President Jefferson Davis and his family lived here from 1861 to 1865. After the Civil War, the house became United States Military Headquarters District No. One of Virginia, later a public school, and finally, in 1896, a museum.

Exhibits from the 13 Confederate states make this the greatest repository of Confederate artifacts and documents in the world. Some of the treasured artifacts include the original Great Seal of the Confederate States of America, the sword and uniform worn by Robert E. Lee at the surrender at Appomattox Court House, Jefferson Davis's Colt revolver, and the furniture used in the Confederate Executive Mansion during the Civil War. There are also numerous displays of original historical maps, letters, uniforms, flags, firearms, and military equipment.

Open 10 to 5 Monday through Saturday, 1 to 5 Sunday. Closed all major holidays. Admission charge. Gift shop.

Pocahontas State Park (southwest of Richmond on U.S. 360, southeast on VA 655). Almost 2,000 acres provide fishing, boat launch and rentals, hiking, bicycling, picnicking, and swimming. Cabins, tent and trailer sites (April through November).

Admission charge. For more information, phone (804) 796-4255.

Edgar Allan Poe Museum (1914 E. Main St.). Edgar Allan Poe lived and worked in this vicinity for 26 years but is not believed to have occupied this house. Orphaned in 1812, he was given a home and educated by John Allan, of Richmond. Poe left Richmond after a quarrel with Allan, but returned in 1835 to become an editor of the *Southern Literary Messenger,* an important focus for Southern writing. Throughout the years his writings brought him fame, but little money; he died in Baltimore in 1849.

The museum features an audiovisual program, a large scale-model of Richmond as Poe knew it from about 1809 to 1849, and rare Poe relics. On display are the secretary-desk from his office in the Southern Literary Messenger Building, his walking cane, copies of autographed letters and manuscripts, and a record of his distinguished military record, which included an appointment to the U.S. Military Academy at West Point. Poe also spent a year at the University of Virginia. There are possessions here from the home of Poe's foster mother, Mrs. Frances Valentine Allan, and relics belonging to his wife. The Raven Room displays more than 40 James Carling illustrations for Poe's famous poem, "The Raven."

Adjacent to the Poe Museum is a converted carriage house and the 1737 Old Stone House, the oldest house still standing in Richmond. Furnishings are mid-18th century, and artifacts found here in archæological digs date from 1675 to 1875.

Open 10 to 4 Tuesday through Saturday, 1:30 to 4 Sunday and Monday. Closed Christmas Day. Admission charge.

Richmond Children's Museum (740 N. Sixth St.). This unique museum of hands-on exhibits was designed for children from two to twelve years old.

Open Tuesdays through Sundays. Closed Mondays, Fourth of July, Thanksgiving, Christmas, and New Year's Day.

Saint John's Episcopal Church (E. Broad and 24th streets). Patrick Henry's famous "Give me liberty or give me death" speech was given in this 1741 church. It was the only church in Richmond until 1814.

Guided tours daily. Closed Thanksgiving, December 24, 25, 31, and New Year's Day. Admission charge.

Saint Paul's Episcopal Church (Nine and Grace streets). Built in 1845, this church was attended by Jefferson Davis, president of the Confederate states, and Gen. Robert E. Lee. Davis was here attending services when word came of Lee's surrender.

Open 10 to 4 Monday through Saturday, 1 to 4 Sunday. Closed holidays.

Science Museum of Virginia (2500 W. Broad St.). Planetarium programs, Omnimax films, computer exhibits, and hands-on displays make this museum entertaining as well as informative.

State Capitol (Capitol Square, Nine and Grace streets). Designed by Thomas Jefferson after a Roman temple located in Nîmes, France, the capitol building was begun in 1785. The General Assembly of Virginia, the oldest lawmaking body in the western hemisphere (its first session was in the church at Jamestown in 1619, more than one year before the Pilgrims landed at Plymouth Rock), first met here in 1788. The building served as the Confederate Capitol from 1861 to 1865.

The guided tour begins in the entrance hall, where Thomas Jefferson's original plaster model of the building is on view. The Rotunda is famous for its beautiful interior dome, which arches over Houdon's white marble statue of George Washington, the only one for which he ever posed. The restored hall of the House of Delegates is filled with life-sized pieces of statuary of such prominent figures as Robert E. Lee, Henry Clay, Patrick Henry, and Sam Houston. It was in this very room in 1807 that Aaron Burr was tried for treason and acquitted, with Chief Justice of the United States John Marshall presiding. Gen. Robert E. Lee stood here on April 23, 1861, and accepted command of the Confederate armed forces of Virginia. The former Senate Chamber, now used as a hearing room, contains paintings depicting the establishment of the first permanent English settlement in America and a scene from the siege of Yorktown.

Open free daily 9 to 5, April through November; 9 to 5 Monday through Saturday and 1 to 5 Sunday, December through March. Closed Thanksgiving, Christmas, and New Year's Day.

Valentine Museum (1015 E. Clay St.). Three separate buildings house this museum: the Wickham-Valentine House, built in 1812 by the lawyer who successfully defended Aaron Burr; the Bransford Cecil House, built in 1840 and moved to this site in 1954; and a row of three Victorian town houses, the Gray-Valentine Houses, built around 1870. There is a guided tour through the Wickham-Valentine House, a beautiful structure elegantly furnished in 19th-century style. The other buildings contain collections of historic artifacts, and a particularly interesting display of old photographs showing life in early Richmond.

Open 10 to 5, Tuesday through Saturday, 1:30 to 5 Sunday. Closed holidays. Admission charge.

Virginia Historical Society (428 North Blvd.). Popularly known as Battle Abbey, this building is the official headquarters of the Virginia Historical Society. The exhibit galleries contain collections of Confederate weapons, uniforms, military equipment, and battle flags, as well as a celebrated display of murals depicting scenes from the Civil War.

Open 9 to 5 Monday through Friday, 2 to 5 Saturday. Closed holidays. Admission charge.

Virginia House (4301 Sulgrave Rd., 1/4 mile off VA 147, Cary Street). Built in 1125 by England's first Earl of Warwick, this elegant Tudor residence is constructed of materials from the Priory of the Holy Sepulchre at Warwick. The building was rebuilt as a residence in 1565 and moved here in 1925. The west wing is modeled after Sulgrave Manor, at one time the home of Lawrence Washington.

Furnishings are authentic period pieces—old tapestries, velvet upholstered furniture, armor from the Tower of London, and the original painted glass window installed to commemorate a visit here by Queen Elizabeth in 1572.

Open daily by appointment only. Phone (804) 353-4251. Admission charge.

Virginia Museum of Fine Arts (Boulevard and Grove Avenue). Valuable collections of art from all over the world are on display in this museum, America's first state-supported arts institution. The museum is noted for its collection of Fabergé jewelry, Russian Easter eggs, paintings by Monet and Goya, and Art Nouveau works. Both classical and contemporary plays are performed October through April by a repertory company.

Open 11 to 5 Tuesday through Saturday, 1 to 5 Sunday. Closed Mondays, Fourth of July, Thanksgiving, Christmas, and New Year's Day. Admission charge.

Wilton (S. Wilton Road, off Cary Street, 8 miles west of Richmond). William Randolph III built this Georgian brick residence in 1750. It was moved from its original location by the James River to Wilton Road in 1935 and now serves as the headquarters of the National Society of Colonial Dames in Virginia. Distinguished visitors here included Washington, Lafayette, Thomas Jefferson (whose mother was a Randolph), and Benjamin Harrison V of Berkeley, who was Mrs. Randolph's brother and a signer of the Declaration of Independence. The interior of the residence is completely paneled and contains 18th-century furniture and portraits.

Open Tuesday through Sunday. By appointment in August. Closed holidays and on Sundays in July. Phone (804) 282-5936. Admission charge.

Richmond National Battlefield Park

On April 1, 1865, Grant broke through Lee's lines at Petersburg in another attempt to capture the capital of the Confederate states at Richmond. Outnumbered, Lee sent word to the Confederate government that he would no longer be able to defend the city, and with his starving army began a weary retreat to escape the closely pursuing Federals. Upon reaching Appomattox Court House, Lee's army found itself completely surrounded. On April 9, 1865, one week after the fall of Richmond, Lee met with Grant and signed the surrender papers that signaled the end of the Civil War.

Two of the attempts to capture Richmond were in the 800-acre area of this park, and a complete tour of the battlefields requires a 57-mile drive. The Visitor Center has an audiovisual program and museum exhibits on the campaigns of the Seven Days, the Siege, and Cold Harbor, a savage battle where Grant saw 7,000 of his men fall in 30 minutes. Free maps and interpretive markers guide visitors along the tour of restored field fortifications, houses, and forts.

Main Visitor Center at 3215 E. Broad St., in Chimborazo Park, on U.S. 60 east in Richmond. Free; open daily 9 to 5. Closed Christmas and New Year's Day. Free visitors centers with museums are also located at Cold Harbor (unstaffed), 16 miles northeast on VA 156, open daily during daylight hours; and Fort Harrison, 10 miles southeast on VA 5 and Park Entrance Road, open daily 9:30 to 5:30 June through August.

Roanoke

Barn Dinner Theatre (6071 Airport Rd.). A professional cast gives Broadway performances here at this quaint theatre-in-the-round.

For reservations, phone (703) 387-2276.

Mill Mountain Theatre (Center in the Square, 1 Market Square). Live theatre productions offer summer seasons of entertainment, with productions ranging from Agatha Christie mysteries to Rogers and Hart musical comedies.

Performances nightly except Mondays. Matinees Saturdays and Sundays, December through August. Special events September through November. For reservations, write: Mill Mountain Theatre, P.O. Box 505, Roanoke, VA 24003, or phone (703) 342-5740 or 342-5743.

Mill Mountain Zoological Park (off VA 220, I-581, and Blue Ridge Parkway). Lion cubs, ocelots, giant tortoises, and kinkajous live in this children's zoo in the story-book houses of Billy Goat Gruff Castle, Farmer Brown's Barnyard, Mary Had a Little Lamb, and the Three Pigs.

A miniature train ride circles the entire zoo. Children can have birthday parties in the Tree House; for reservations, phone (703) 343-3241.

Open daily May through October. Admission charge. Snack bar, picnic area.

Science Museum of Western Virginia (1 Market Square). Exhibits here explore the different areas of science, from energy conservation to live marine animals. Planetarium shows.

Open daily except Mondays. Closed holidays. Admission charge.

Virginia Museum of Transportation (303 Norfolk Ave., downtown). The South's largest collection of steam locomotives is housed here, as well as one of the largest model railroad layouts in the country. There are exhibits of other modes of transportation, including covered wagons, buggies, and automobiles, and an old-timey railroad station offers railroad exhibits.

Open daily. Admission charge.

Booker T. Washington National Monument (18 miles south of Roanoke on VA 116 to Burnt Chimney, then 6 miles east on VA 122). Booker T. Washington, American black educator and advisor of presidents, was born a slave on this small tobacco plantation, now a national monument, near Roanoke, Virginia. He and his family were freed in 1865, and moved to Malden, West Virginia. Determined to get an education, Washington worked at a salt furnace and in a coal mine, then made a 400-mile trek at the age of 16 to attend Hampton Institute. After graduation he taught for two years, and in 1881 founded Tuskegee Institute at Tuskegee, Alabama. When not occupied with his duties as principal, Washington lectured widely, urging blacks to achieve true independence through acquiring an education. He died in 1915; his autobiography, *Up from Slavery*, was published in 1901.

The Visitor Center contains exhibits on Washington's life, a film, and free maps for the self-guided walking tour. On the grounds of the 224-acre plantation are a slave cabin, tobacco barn, and other reconstructed farm buildings. Daily mid-June through Labor Day attendants in 19th-century farm dress perform colonial farm chores as they were done during Washington's lifetime.

Open, free, daily 8:30 to 5. Closed Thanksgiving, Christmas, and New Year's Day. Picnic area.

Salem

Dixie Caverns (5 miles west of Salem, exit 39 off I-81). The only caverns in southwest Virginia, these have mirror pools and fantastically shaped limestone formations; there is a 45-minute conducted tour. Adjoining the caverns are pottery and mineral shops (mineral shop open May through September). Also adjacent are camping facilities, open April through mid-October.

Open daily 8 to 10 P.M. June through Labor Day, to 5 P.M. the rest of the year. Closed December 20 through 25. Admission charge.

Lakeside Amusement Park (1526 E. Main St., exit 41 off I-81). This giant amusement park contains dozens of rides and country-music shows.

Open 10 to 10 Sunday through Friday and 9 A.M. to midnight, May 20 through Labor Day; 10 to 10 weekends only April through late May and after Labor Day through September. Admission charge. Picnic area.

Schuyler

The long-running television series, "The Waltons," was based on author Earl Hamner's recollections of growing up here in his rural hometown.

Shenandoah National Park

The beauty of this heavily wooded parkland and wildlife sanctuary attracts thousands of visitors annually. The park has much to offer to the visitor: camping, horseback riding,

The Blue Ridge Mountains, from Shenandoah National Park

backpacking, picnicking, and miles of scenic trails to explore. Orientation programs, museums, exhibits, maps, and information are available at the Byrd Visitor Center (open daily March through December, Saturdays and Sundays January and February), located south of Luray, Milepost 51; and Dickey Ridge Visitor Center (open daily April through October), located south of Front Royal, Milepost 4.6. The visitor centers are open daily from 9 A.M. to 5 P.M., except for winter closures.

Accommodations in the park range from camping and trailer sites to furnished cottages and mountain lodges. For reservations and information write: Park Concessioner, ARA-Virginia Skyline Company, Inc., P.O. Box 727, Luray, VA 22835. Or phone for lodge accommodations: the Skyland Lodge or Big Meadows Lodge, (703) 999-2221; December through March phone (703) 743-5108. Lodge and cottage accommodations are available April through October; winter months only at Big Meadows Lodge. Another park concessioner maintains six trail cabins for hikers. Advance reservations must be obtained; write Potomac Appalachian Trail Club, 1718 North Street, N.W., Washington, D.C. 20036.

For other park information, write: Shenandoah Valley Travel Association, P.O. Box 488, New Market, VA 22844. For a recording on weather conditions, open campgrounds and fees, required permits, etc., phone (703) 999-2266; for further information, phone (703) 999-2229. The park has a vehicle entrance fee.

Shenandoah River Canoe Trips. Breathtaking scenery, abundant wildlife, searching for Indian artifacts, fishing, and cave exploring are among the attractions of canoe trips down the Shenandoah River. Completely outfitted trips are available, including transportation back to your car at the put-in, guide service, bait and tackle for fishing, overnight equipment, and even a steak dinner, if you wish.

For details, write or phone: Downriver Canoe Company, Route 1, Box 256A, Bentonville, VA 22610, or phone (703) 635-5526; or Shenandoah River Outfitters, Inc., RFD 3, Luray, VA 22835, phone (703) 743-4159 (available upon request, bluegrass music, hayrides, steak dinners, lunches).

Skyline Drive (junction with U.S. 340, south of Front Royal; I-66W junction 4 miles north). Skyline Drive winds its way through the Shenandoah National Park for 105 miles, following the crest of the Blue Ridge Mountains and traversing the 300 square miles of the park. More than 70 overlooks along the way provide views of the Shenandoah River Valley to the west and the Piedmont to the east. At the southern terminus of the Skyline Drive, the scenic Blue Ridge Parkway begins (see *Afton Mountain*).

Numbered mileposts indicate stopping sites with special features (northbound, beginning at Front Royal):

(Mile 4.6) **Dickey Ridge Visitor Center.** Ranger information, picnic area, programs, exhibits. Open daily April through October.

(Mile 22.2) **Matthews Arm.** Tent and trailer sites (no hookups), picnic facilities, restrooms. Open May through mid-October.

(Mile 24.1) **Elkwallow Wayside.** Snack bar, gas, campstore, trout fishing, picnic area. Open daily May through October.

(Mile 31.5) **Panorama.** Coffee shop, gift and craft shop, service station, trout fishing. Open April through November.

(Mile 41.7) **Skyland Lodge.** Accommodations, dining room, tap room, trout fishing, horseback riding, lawn games. Open April through October.

(Mile 51.1) **Byrd Visitor Center.** Museum, information, programs. Open daily March through December, Saturdays and Sundays January and February.

(Mile 51.3) **Big Meadows.** Tent and trailer sites (no hookups), showers, restrooms, grocery store, wagon rides, picnic facilities, trout fishing. Closed January and February. **Big Meadows Wayside.** Coffee shop, service station, campstore. Open daily. **Big Meadows Lodge.** Accommodations, dining room, tap room, horseback riding, bicycling. Open mid-May through October; motel rooms open November through March only.

(Mile 57.6) **Lewis Mountain.** Tent and trailer sites (no hookups), restrooms, picnic facilities, trout fishing. Open mid-May through October. Cottages, campstore, laundry, shower facilities open April through October.

(Mile 62.9) **South River.** Round trip to falls, 2 1/2 miles; picnic grounds.

(Mile 79.5) **Loft Mountain.** Tent and trailer sites (no hookups), picnic facilities, restrooms. Open April through October. Restaurant, campstore, service station open June through October.

There are four main entrances to the park along the Skyline Drive:

North Entrance (Front Royal) from I-66, U.S. 340, VA 55, and VA 522.

Thornton Gap (Mile 31.6) from U.S. 211.

Swift Run Gap (Mile 65.7) from U.S. 33.

South Entrance (Rockfish Gap) from I-64, U.S. 250, and the Blue Ridge Parkway.

The park roads and facilities may occasionally close in inclement weather.

Smithfield

Picturesque Smithfield, once a thriving shipping port overlooking the Pagan River, is now a processing center for pork products and the home of the famous Smithfield ham. The Smithfield Inn here is famed for its fine dining. The walking tour around the town includes more than 30 buildings of interest, from Church Street mansions, graceful old Victorian homes, and a gingerbread cottage, to buildings dating from the 18th century to pre-Civil War times. The Isle of Wight Courthouse was built 1750-51, the Gaming House prior to 1766, and the Clerk's Office and County Jail in 1799.

For a fee, guided tours are available. For a brochure, phone (804) 357-7131.

Saint Luke's Church (2 miles south of Smithfield, on VA 10). Historic Saint Luke's, our nation's oldest standing church, was built in 1632. It is also the only original Gothic church in the United States, inspired by our forefathers' memory of the great cathedrals of Europe. Saint Luke's is a national historic landmark; it has no clergy, although services are held on Easter, Thanksgiving, and Christmas, with the public invited.

The original wood-and-parchment lantern still hangs above the entrance door of the church. As visitors enter, they have to step over the wide, wooden doorsill, placed there centuries ago by the colonists to keep out animals and to make worshipers enter reverently, stooped in the attitude of prayer. Gracing the interior are the church's original candlesticks and brass alms box and basins, 350-year-old altar tapestry, and a 17th-century baptismal basin, made from the silver of coins melted down and set in a font hewn and shaped from a single oak log. The church also possesses a small, priceless organ with gold-plated keys, made in 1665 and said to be one of only three like it in the world. Two marble tombstones dating back to the 1600s are buried in the floor near the altar.

Open, free, 9 to 5 daily. Closed Christmas and January. Guided tours.

Smithfield Inn (112 E. Main St., at junction of VA 10 and VA 258). Stop at the Smithfield Inn for lunch or an overnight stay while touring Bacon's Castle and Saint Luke's Church. This small, quaint inn, tucked back on a shaded street, was established in 1752. It still has the original mantels, paneling, cupboards, and stairway, and each room has period furnishings. The dining room specializes in Brunswick Stew and the famous Smithfield ham.

Lunch 11:30 to 2 Tuesday through Saturday; dinner 5 to 8:30 Tuesday through Thursday, until 9 P.M. Friday and Saturday, 12 to 8 Sundays. Dining and room reservations suggested; write Smithfield Inn, 112 E. Main St., Smithfield, VA 23430, or phone (804) 357-4358. Closed Mondays and December 25 through January 2.

South Boston

Staunton River State Park (8 miles northeast of South Boston on VA 304, then 11 miles southeast on VA 344). More than 1,000 acres of parkland with a long shoreline on Buggs Island Lake offer fishing, boat rentals and ramp, waterskiing, swimming (in one of the state's largest outdoor pools), tennis courts, picnic facilities, a playground, and nature trails. Six cabins (May through September), tent and trailer sites (April through November). Concession, Visitor Center with evening programs.

For more information, phone (804) 572-4623.

Staunton

Staunton is the home of Mary Baldwin College, an old Presbyterian-related four-year liberal arts college. Trinity Episcopal Church (214 W. Beverley St.) is built on the same site as the original church that served for 16 days in 1781 as the Revolutionary capitol of the state.

For more information, contact the Chamber of Commerce, 30 N. New St., Staunton, VA 24401, or phone Travel Information Service, (703) 885-8504.

Gypsy Hill Park (off Thornrose and Churchville avenues). This park offers tennis, softball, basketball, miniature train ride, golf, picnicking, a zoo, playground, and fairgrounds. Swimming is permissible late May through Labor Day. The lake is stocked with fish.

Park open, free, daily; charge for some attractions.

Cyrus McCormick Memorial Wayside (16 miles southwest of Staunton via U.S. 11, I-81; one mile east of I-81 on VA 606 near Steele's Tavern). Cyrus McCormick, inventor of the grain reaper in 1831, was born in Walnut Grove. His reaper introduced the era of farm mechanization by increasing the speed of harvesting grain five times over that of the old sickle or scythe method, and with a fraction of the effort. A wayside park houses the old gristmill and blacksmith shop where he developed the reaper, and tells the story of its development.

Free; open 8 to 5 daily, April through November; summers until dusk.

Museum of American Frontier Culture (1 mile west of Staunton on VA 644, exit 57). Eighteenth-century farmsteads of Appalachia, Germany, England, and Northern Ireland have been re-created as they were in the early settlement days of the Shenandoah Valley.

Open daily. Closed Christmas and New Year's Day. Admission charge.

Woodrow Wilson Birthplace (on U.S. 11, 24 N. Coalter St.). Thomas Woodrow Wilson, president of Princeton University in 1902, governor of New Jersey, and 28th president of the United States, was born here in what was then the manse of the First Presbyterian Church. The imposing, three-story Greek Revival home is furnished with family pieces, and a film presents Wilson's achievements as president, including his "Fourteen Points" for peace that gave birth to the League of Nations.

The 19th-century Victorian Town Garden is charmingly restored. On display here is Wilson's presidential Pierce-Arrow limousine. Wilson subsequently bought the automobile for the original purchase price of $3,000, and used it daily until his death in 1924.

Open 9 to 5 daily; until 6 P.M. in summer. Closed Sundays in January through February, and on Thanksgiving, Christmas, and New Year's Day. Admission charge.

Strasburg

Strasburg Museum (E. King Street). The former Southern Railway depot, originally built as a steam pottery, houses this museum. It features 18th- and 19th-century artifacts from the local farming community, plus numerous Indian artifacts and fossils.

Open daily 10 to 4, May through October. Admission charge.

Surry

Bacon's Castle (7 1/2 miles southeast of Surry on VA 10, then 1/2 mile northeast on VA 617). Built in 1655, this house was once occupied by Virginia rebels under the direction of Nathaniel Bacon, protesting the tyrannical rule of Royal Governor William Berkeley. It is from this occupation that Bacon's Castle derived its name. There is an audiovisual program on the house's history, followed by a guided tour. William and Mary 17th-century English furniture graces the interior. One interesting piece is a wooden "field" bed, so-named because it could be disassembled, put on a cart, and reassembled for an officer's use in the battlefield. A windowpane has a love poem etched on it by the owner to his wife in 1840, which reads in part: "Thou art but a little tablet on which to inscribe a record of human happiness and yet these words may be found here even after both of us have been laid in the dust so uncertain is everything connected with human life."

Open 10 to 5 Wednesday through Sunday, last week in April through September. Admission charge.

Chippokes Plantation State Park (6 miles east of Surry via VA 10, then on to VA 633). Chippokes, named in honor of an Indian chief who befriended the early Jamestown settlers, has been a working farm for more than 350 years and has retained its original 1,400-acre boundaries since 1619. The large, antebellum mansion was built in 1854 and is an excellent example of the pre-Civil War plantation house found throughout the South. Furnishings reflect plantation life from the 17th through 20th centuries.

An inheritance of the Civil War period is the "Widow's Room," a small room at the top of a steep and winding staircase. Such quarters provided privacy and a place where women could keep vigil while they waited for the safe return of their husbands.

The 18th-century brick kitchen, built separate from the main house to keep down heat and the danger of fire, contains early cooking artifacts. There are several outbuildings, including one containing a coach believed to be more than 200 years old. The six-acre formal garden has one of the largest crepe myrtle arrangements on the East Coast. Recreational facilities include a public fishing area, bicycle rentals, and bridle, walking, and bicycle paths. Picnic area. Visitor Center.

Open 10 to 6 Tuesday through Sunday, Memorial Day through Labor Day. Admission charge.

Smith's Fort Plantation (2 miles north of Surry). The property upon which this house was built originally was a gift from Chief Powhatan to his daughter, Pocahontas, when she married John Rolfe in 1614. Their son, Thomas Rolfe, eventually sold the land in 1652 to Thomas Warren, who built the present brick house, one of the oldest in Virginia. It received its name from Smith's Fort, built here in 1609 by the Jamestown settlers. Remains of the breastworks of the fort are within walking distance, and the house's secret underground exit there, built in case of an Indian attack, is shown during the conducted tour.

The furnishings of the home, many with dates carved in them, include such rare pieces as a 1555 dispatch case, a 1603 chair with the original petit point, and a 1709 chest. A favorite among visitors is a 17th-century student's chair, made with a forward tilt so that a student inattentive enough to fall asleep would slide off! In the basement are a loom and spinning wheel more than 300 years old.

Open 10 to 5 Wednesday through Sunday, last week in April through September. Admission charge.

Tangier Island

Capt. John Smith explored this small island, located 12 miles out in Chesapeake Bay, and gave it its name in 1607. It was settled by a family named West, who bought the island from the Indians for two overcoats, and in 1686 was purchased by John Crockett, a Cornish fisherman who moved here with his family.

During the War of 1812, the British established headquarters at Tangier and impressed all the young men and their boats into service, but during the night the women sank all the small boats, and the British were forced to sail without the men.

The island has an airfield, and excursion boats make daily trips seasonally. The island offers swimming, fishing, duck hunting, and quiet strolls through a village where no automobiles are allowed and most of the inhabitants still speak with an Elizabethan accent. Accommodations are available at the Islander Tourist Home and the Chesapeake House; for reservations phone (804) 891-2331. The Chesapeake House specializes in family-style meals of homemade bread, corn pudding, crab, and ham dishes. A small museum, located in the Town Hall, features exhibits of local history.

Tangier Island and Chesapeake Bay Cruises. Narrated cruises are offered on modern cruise ships equipped with air-conditioned lounges, sun decks, and snack bars.

Departures, Tangier and Chesapeake Cruises from Reedville, Virginia, and Tangier Ferry Service from Pier G, Somers Cove Marina, Crisfield, Maryland. Reservations required; write Tangier and Chesapeake Cruises, Inc., Warsaw, VA 22572, phone (804) 333-4656.

Departures daily May through September. Trips 1 1/2 hours each way, and two hours on the island.

Tappahannock

Capt. John Smith landed here in 1608, but was driven back to his ship by local Indians. A warehouse and trading post were established in the early 1600s by Jacob Hobbs, and for many years this area was known as "Hobbs His Hole." Eventually the town was given the Indian name Tappahannock, meaning "on the rise and fall of water," for its location next to a river.

A walking tour through the town includes 13 old homes

and buildings, among them a clerk's office, debtor's prison, customhouse, and courthouse, all built between 1728 and 1750.

Outstanding family dining is offered at Lowery's Seafood Restaurant on Route 17. Open daily 6 A.M. to 9 P.M., from 7 A.M. Sundays (until 3 P.M. only Christmas Eve). Closed Christmas Day.

Triangle

Prince William Forest Park (1/4 west of Triangle on VA 619). Camping, picnicking, hiking, and park ranger service are available in the 12,000-acre area of this park.

For more information, phone (703) 221-7181.

Tysons Corner

One of the largest shopping centers in the country is located in this Virginia suburban area of Washington, D.C.

Urbanna

The town of Urbanna was formed in 1673 and named for the English shire. It began primarily as a port, with steamboats providing the major link with big cities. Piracy was a constant threat in the early years. The town also suffered from pillaging during the Revolution, and again in 1812–14 and the Civil War.

Today, local watermen provide the principal industry of Urbanna, with a steady supply of oysters, crab, and fish from the famous Rappahannock River.

The town's major claim to fame is the annual Urbanna Oyster Festival, held the first weekend in November. Thousands of visitors gather for the two-day celebration to sample from the numerous street booths offering arts, crafts, and oysters . . . fried, frittered, stewed, roasted, or raw. Other foods, music, and activities make the festival a real event, which culminates in a town parade.

Virginia Beach

Capt. John Smith landed here on April 26, 1607, on what is now a renowned seashore playground. Virginia Beach offers miles of boardwalk and beach, sun, sand, surf, luxury hotels, and fine restaurants. A self-guided motor tour features nationally recognized landmarks, with helpful roadside markers along the route. For more information, write: Virginia Beach Visitors Bureau, 19th and Pacific Avenue, P.O. Box 200, Virginia Beach, VA 23458, or phone (800) 446-8038.

Cape Henry Memorial and Lighthouse (6 miles north of Virginia Beach on U.S. 60). A memorial cross here in Fort Story Military Reservation marks the site of the colonists' first landing in Virginia on April 26, 1607. The settlers set up a cross "at Chesupioc Bay," and named the site Cape Henry for Henry, then Prince of Wales, the oldest son of King James I. Several days later the settlers sailed up the James River and established a permanent settlement at Jamestown, Virginia's capital for 92 years.

Nearby is an octagonal stone lighthouse, built in 1791–92, the first lighthouse authorized and constructed by the U.S. government. The building stone was mined in the Aquia Quarries, which provided stone for the White House, the Capitol Building, and Mount Vernon. The original lighthouse was replaced by a more modern facility in 1881.

Free; open daily. Visitor passes issued at Fort Story gate. On the Sunday closest to April 26, a commemorative service is held here, reenacting the colonists' landing.

Little Creek Naval Amphibious Base (on Shore Drive between Independence Boulevard and Diamond Springs Road). Visitors are invited to go aboard an "Open House" ship and visit the Amphibious Museum.

Free; open 1 to 5 P.M. Saturday and Sunday; passes at the Main Gate.

Lynnhaven House (8 miles north off U.S 225 on Wishart Road). This historic house has been almost continuously occupied since it was first built in the late 1600s. Except for minor repairs, it stands virtually unchanged today. The interior contains period furnishings; on the grounds are a small herb garden, farm animals, and 19th-century graveyard. The fence around the grounds was made by the attendants here, using old rail-splitting tools.

Open 10 to 5 Tuesday through Saturday, 1 to 5 Sunday, April through October. Closed Mondays. Admission charge.

Maritime Historical Museum (24th Street and Oceanfront). Many nautical displays and relics are exhibited in this historic Life-Saving/Coast Guard Station.

Open daily Memorial Day through October. Closed Mondays rest of year. Closed December 24, 25, 31, and New Year's Day. Admission charge.

Nimmo United Methodist Church (Triangle and Woodhouse Corner roads). The oldest Methodist church in America, built in 1791, it still has in use today its original pine floor, boxed pews, and slave balcony.

Seashore State Park (5 miles north on U.S. 60, near Cape Henry). This park of nearly 3,000 acres offers nature trails, bicycle paths, boating, swimming, fishing, water-skiing, and programs at its Visitor Center. Facilities include cabins (May through September) and trailer and tent sites (March through November).

For more information, phone (804) 481-2131. Admission charge.

Thoroughgood House (off U.S. 13, Northampton Boulevard, 1636 Parish Rd.). The builder of this house, Mr. Adam Thoroughgood, was one of Virginia's earliest settlers. Credited with naming Norfolk, he was also responsible for bringing George Washington's great-great-grandfather to America.

Thoroughgood House is one of the oldest brick homes still standing in America. Close inspection of its original interior plaster walls still reveals the bits of animal hair and oyster shells used by the builder to give the plaster substance. Seventeenth-century furnishings include a mirror with the original glass, massive sideboard bearing the carved date 1684, and an unusual "press cupboard" where clothes were tightly packed in drawers to smooth out wrinkles.

A charming, 17th-century gentleman's pleasure garden surrounds the house. The two small, hand-carved animals atop poles on either side of the walk were placed here by the family to bring them good luck. The house's bricks, hand-made, still reveal paw prints where the family dog ran across them before they were dried.

Open 10 to 5 Tuesday through Saturday, 11 to 5 Sunday, April through December; 12 to 5 Tuesday through Saturday, January through March. Closed Fourth of July, Thanksgiving, Christmas, and New Year's Day. Admission charge.

Virginia Marine Science Museum (717 General Booth Blvd.). Virginia's marine environment is presented here in aquarium displays and hands-on exhibits.

Open daily. Closed Christmas and New Year's Day. Admission charge.

Warm Springs

Waterwheel Restaurant and Inn (at Gristmill Square, two blocks west of Route 220). This delightful restaurant is housed in a mill located on the same site as the original mill built in 1771. Diners can choose from veal, fresh trout, garden-grown vegetables, and home-baked desserts. Beverages are served from the tiny, authentically furnished English Pub.

The inn offers rooms with fireplaces and kitchen facilities, if desired. Swimming pool, sauna, tennis courts, riding, and snow-skiing in season.

Dinner 6 to 9 P.M. Tuesday through Thursday (Friday and Saturday to 10 P.M.); lunch only 11 A.M. to 2 P.M. Sundays. Closed Mondays, Fourth of July, December 25, and the first two weeks in March. Reservations suggested; for dining phone (703) 839-2311, for lodging (703) 839-2231.

Warrenton

Picturesquely nestled in the foothills of the Blue Ridge Mountains, Warrenton's old homes and historical buildings provide a pleasant stroll about the town. For more information, write the Warrenton/Fauquier Chamber of Commerce, Box 127, or phone (703) 347-4414.

Flying Circus Aerodrome (7 miles south on U.S. 15, then 4 miles southeast on U.S. 17 near Bealeton). Pilots flying vintage planes from World War I to II perform aerobatic maneuvers, have mock "dogfights," perform parachute jumps, and give other demonstrations.

Open 2:30 to 4 Sundays, May through October. Admission charge. Picnic area.

George Washington Birthplace National Monument

(On the Potomac River, 38 miles southeast of Fredericksburg on VA 3, then 2 miles east on VA 204). George Washington was born here February 11, 1732, on his father's 1,500-acre tidewater plantation on the banks of the Potomac. When he was three he moved to what would later be known as the Mount Vernon Plantation, but he often returned here to visit his elder half brother, who had inherited the farm upon the death of their father.

The original house burned to the ground on Christmas Day 1779 and a memorial house, constructed of bricks made of clay taken from a nearby field, was built on the old foundations. No records of the details of the original house's construction have ever been found, and the existing building is patterned after the typical Virginia plantation home of its time. Furnishings are period pieces 200 to 300 years old; the only original piece here that escaped the 1779 fire is a small tea table.

Lost colonial crafts come to life on the plantation today, and every effort is made to reproduce for the visitor the sights, sounds, and smells as they would have been experienced by young George Washington. Costumed hostesses cook colonial dishes over open fireplaces, brew medicines, prepare soap from animal fat and fireplace ashes, and make candles from string dipped repeatedly into hot wax. From sheep raised on the farm, they card and spin wool, dye it in crushed flower and berry juice, and weave it into patterns on a loom. In the farm's workshop, men forge nails, build farm equipment, and even make shoes. All the herbs, flowers, and food used in the kitchen are grown on the farm from varieties common in the 18th century. Even the livestock and poultry are colonial varieties, and the fields are plowed using the Washington family's 2,000-pound Devon breed of cattle.

A short drive leads to the family burial grounds, where Washington's father, grandfather, great-grandfather, and 29 other members of his family are laid to rest.

Free; open daily 9 to 5, summer weekends until 6:30 P.M. Closed Christmas and New Year's Day. Visitor Center offers a film and museum exhibits. Picnic area.

West Point

Mattaponi Indian Museum (on the Mattaponi Indian Reservation, 13 miles west on VA 30). This museum is operated by the Mattaponi Tribe Indians, the last remnant of one of the 32 tribes ruled by Chief Powhatan, father of Pocahontas. The Mattaponi Reservation consists of about 125 acres; proceeds from the museum and gift shop supplement the tribe's income. Of historical interest are the tomahawk wielded by Chief Opecancanough in the massacre of Jamestown settlers in 1622 and 1644, and a necklace worn by Princess Pocahontas in 1607. A 150-year-old buckskin suit, stone scalping knives, hefty three-pound war clubs, beaded medicine bag, and curious stones shaped like feet and used by the Indians to fit moccasins are among the other displays.

Open 10 to 6 daily. Admission charge. Picnic area. Hunting and fishing guides available; dirt boat ramp at the Mattaponi River.

Williamsburg

The first settlement here was a stockade, built by Jamestown colonists in 1633 to guard against Indian attacks. It was still just a stockade settlement in 1693 when a royal charter was granted to Middletown Plantation, as the settlement was called, for the establishment of the College of William and Mary, second oldest college (after Harvard) in the United States. When the statehouse at Jamestown was destroyed by fire in 1699 and the state capital was moved here, the town was pushed into prominence and renamed Williamsburg, in honor of King William III.

In a daring move in May 1776, the Virginia Convention demonstrated its support of the Continental Congress in Philadelphia by hauling down the British flag from the Williamsburg capitol building and raising the Grand Union, the new flag of the colonies. Every May 15 this event is re-enacted in Williamsburg; the Grand Union then flies until July 4. From 1776 to 1780, Williamsburg served as the American Revolution's wartime capital. Cornwallis had his headquarters here for a time, as did Washington and Rochambeau. The Governor's Palace and the College of William and Mary provided makeshift hospitals for the wounded, carted here the 12 miles from Yorktown by wagon.

After 1780, when the capital was moved to Richmond, Williamsburg began to decline in importance. The Civil War touched the community briefly in a battle east of town in 1862. Confederate general Joseph Johnston and Union general George McClellan camped here, and Federal troops occupied the town for more than two years.

In 1926, John D. Rockefeller, Jr., made possible the restoration of a large part of the colonial area of Williamsburg. The mile-long Duke of Gloucester Street, scene of some of the most momentous events in the formation of this nation, is the heart of this restoration project. As described by Franklin D. Roosevelt, it is America's most historic avenue. Visitors here today enjoy leisurely carriage rides, stroll through formal gardens, and see historic homes and public buildings restored to their grandeur of more than two centuries ago.

For ease of reference, the attractions of Colonial Williamsburg are listed here first. The attractions of the town of Williamsburg follow and are listed separately. Additionally, there are a number of historic James River plantations located between Williamsburg and Richmond on both

Duke of Gloucester Street, Williamsburg

sides of the James River that are well worth seeing. For more information about these magnificent estates, see *Charles City.*

Colonial Williamsburg

The restored colonial area of Williamsburg is nearly a mile in length and contains 88 original buildings, as well as numerous others that have been carefully reconstructed on their original foundations. The Governor's Palace and 25 buildings—authentically furnished with English and American antiques, and set in almost 100 acres of gardens and greenery (all 18th-century plant varieties)—are open to the public. On the grounds and in the buildings, costumed guides interpret early colonial life, and artisans reenact day-to-day chores. The area offers shops, carriage rides, candlelight concerts and plays, the muster of the militia company, lectures and films, and a host of other special visitor activities.

Colonial Williamsburg Visitor Center (VA 132 and Colonial Parkway). Here visitors may purchase admission tickets;

make lodging, dining, and activities reservations; see historical exhibits and a free orientation film; and take special buses to the Historic Area. For information and a schedule of events, write: The Colonial Williamsburg Foundation, P.O. Box C, Williamsburg, VA 23185, or phone (804) 220-7083. The foundation recommends that guests make lodging and dining reservations well in advance of their visit. Write to: Reservation Office, The Colonial Williamsburg Foundation, P.O. Box C, Williamsburg, VA 23185, or phone (804) 220-7083.

Open, free, daily 8 A.M. to 10 P.M. summers, 9 A.M. to 6 P.M. winters. Cafeteria. Exhibition buildings in the colonial area open daily 9 to 5; to 7 P.M. except Sundays in summer.

Abby Aldrich Rockefeller Folk Art Center (307 S. England St., adjacent to Williamsburg Inn, Historic Area). Changing exhibits of American folk art are exhibited here, as well as art from the museum's permanent collection.

Closed during exhibit changes.

Bassett Hall (York Street). This 18th-century house was once the residence of Mr. and Mrs. John D. Rockefeller, Jr.

Brush-Everard House (east side of Palace Green). This was the home of the town's early mayor. The garden's 150-year-old box plants are the oldest in Williamsburg. The Candlemaker works in the yard, in season.

Bruton Parish Church (corner of Duke of Gloucester Street and Palace Green). This Episcopal church building has the original windows and walls and has been in continuous use since 1715.

The Capitol (end of Duke of Gloucester Street). The House of Burgesses, America's oldest representative assembly, held its meetings here. Great American patriots such as Patrick Henry, George Washington, and George Mason met at this site to pledge their support to the cause of American freedom.

College of William and Mary (west end of Duke of Gloucester Street). The Phi Beta Kappa Society was founded here in 1776. Alumni include James Monroe, Thomas Jefferson, and John Marshall. George Washington served as chancellor for 11 years.

Colonial Dining. Three historic taverns—Christiana Campbell's Tavern, a dining place of George Washington; Chowning's Tavern, an 18th-century alehouse; and King's Arms Tavern, patronized by Patrick Henry and Thomas Jefferson—offer lunch and dinner, served by attendants in colonial costume. Dining reservations recommended; phone Campbell's, (804) 220-7015; Chowning's, (804) 220-7012; or King's Arms, (804) 229-2141.

Courthouse of 1770 (Duke of Gloucester and England streets). This original building served as the seat of local government and was a symbol of law and order for two centuries.

Craft Shops. Craftspeople in colonial costume demonstrate the colonial trades of the bookbinder, wigmaker, bootmaker, printer, silversmith, weaver, baker, milliner, gunsmith, blacksmith, candlemaker, apothecary, and others.

DeWitt Wallace Decorative Arts Gallery (adjoins the Public Hospital). This modern building tastefully displays 18th-century decorative arts.

James Geddy House, Shop, and Foundry (Duke of Gloucester Street and Palace Green). This was the home and workshop of a prominent silversmith.

Governor's Palace and Gardens (Palace Green). Completed in 1720 and destroyed by fire in 1781, this building was referred to as "the Palace" by local townspeople, who objected to the high taxes required to complete its construction. It was the residence of seven royal governors and the first two Virginia governors, Patrick Henry and Thomas Jefferson. Ten acres of restored gardens surround the elegant mansion.

Magazine and Guardhouse (Market Square Green). Arms and ammunition were housed here. The high wall around the building was added when townspeople demanded protection from the possibility of an explosion. Authentic colonial weapons are exhibited and demonstrated.

Public Gaol (Nicholson Street). Criminals and debtors were confined here, as were several of Blackbeard the Pirate's crew in 1718.

Public Hospital. This building is a reconstruction of the first public mental institution in the English colonies.

Raleigh Tavern (Duke of Gloucester Street). This was an important social center where figures such as Washington, Thomas Jefferson, Patrick Henry, and Lafayette often met. A colonial bakery prepares delicacies in the restored kitchen.

Peyton Randolph House (Market Square Green). Peyton Randolph, speaker of the House of Burgesses and president of the First Continental Congress, made this his residence.

Wetherburn's Tavern (Duke of Gloucester Street, near the Capitol). This was a popular tavern and meeting place in its day.

Wren Building (College of William and Mary). Wren Building, dating back to 1695, is still in use; it is the oldest academic building in America.

Wythe House (west side of Palace Green). George Wythe, professor of law and teacher of Thomas Jefferson and John Marshall, had his residence here. George Washington used the house as his headquarters before the siege of Yorktown.

Williamsburg

Anheuser-Busch Hospitality Center (5 miles east of Williamsburg on U.S. 60). The ultramodern Hospitality Center of Anheuser-Busch Brewery is located in a rustic forest setting just outside Busch Gardens. Free monorail ride (runs only when Busch Gardens is open) and color film; pizza, freshly baked Bavarian pretzels, and beer on sale.

Open, free, daily 9 to 4. Closed Thanksgiving, Christmas, and New Year's Day.

Busch Gardens (5 miles east of Williamsburg on U.S. 60) is a replica of the 17th-century "Old Country" of Europe, where more than 300 acres of forestland are subdivided into the continents of England, France, Germany, and Italy. The cobblestoned streets of Merry Olde England lead to a stage show in the replica of Shakespeare's famous Globe Theatre. Cross the moors into Scotland and step aboard the high-speed "Loch Ness Monster" roller coaster. Oompah bands play in a real Oktoberfest Beer Hall in Germany, and rides in Italy are based on the inventions of Leonardo da Vinci. Each country has shows, restaurants, rides, shops, and exhibits. Monorails, excursion boats, sky lifts, and a steam train provide transportation around the park.

Open daily late May through Labor Day; weekends only spring and fall. Hours vary; phone (804) 253-3350 for information. Parking fee. Gate tickets include admission to all rides and attractions except the Shooting Gallery and Arcade.

Carter's Grove Plantation (6 miles southeast on Highway 60). Carter's Grove Plantation was built between 1750 and 1755 by Carter Burwell on a 1,400-acre estate purchased by his grandfather, Robert ("King") Carter. A master woodworker, brought from England by the Carter family, took six years to complete the hand-carved pine interior paneling. Many of the forefathers of the American republic were visitors at Carter's Grove, and legend has it that both Washington and Jefferson proposed marriage to early loves—and were rejected—in the mansion's southwest parlor. Deep scars and the tip of a sword embedded in the stair railing are said to have been made during the Revolution by Colonel Tarleton, a British cavalryman, who hacked the balustrade with his sabre as he rode his horse up the stairway.

The entire width of the stately Georgian mansion is lined with ancient white ash, black locust, and crepe myrtle trees, with a spectacular view of grassy lawns and gardens sloping down to the James River. Hostesses give conducted tours of the restored mansion, rightfully listed as one of the ten most beautiful homes in America.

The Visitor's Information Center exhibits the huge Burwell Family Bible opened to a double page of handwritten records on which are recorded two centuries of family history. A wall map shows a perspective of the Tidewater Region in 1755, including the plantations of that day, and other documents and exhibits trace the history of Carter's Grove.

Open daily 9 to 5 March through November, seasonally during Christmas week. Closed December through February. For information phone (804) 229-1000. Admission charge.

Pottery Factory (5 miles west of Williamsburg, in Lightfoot, on U.S. 60). More than 130 acres of shops and factory outlets offer everything the bargain hunter could want: clothing, shoes, home furnishings, cookware, candles, pewter, brass, crystal, flowers, silverware, gourmet items, prints and frames, Christmas items, Mexican baskets—there is even a greenhouse and more, more, more.

Open, free, daily 8 A.M. to 7 P.M. weekends 8 to 7:30. Closed Christmas Day. Snack bar; restaurant; and cheese, wine, and candy shop.

Williamsburg National Wax Museum (3 miles west of Williamsburg on U.S. 60). Life-size wax figures, set in realistic surroundings, depict historical events in colonial America.

Open 9 A.M. to 9 P.M. June through October, 9 to 5 the rest of the year. Closed Christmas Day. Admission charge.

York River State Park (8 miles northwest of Williamsburg on I-64, Croaker exit; 1 mile north on VA 607, VA 606E). More than 2,000 acres provide hiking, bicycle and nature trails, picnicking, fishing, canoeing, launch for boats, and nature programs.

Open daily. Admission charge.

Winchester

The Pennsylvania Quakers settled in this area in 1732, and 16 years later teenaged George Washington had his first surveying job in Winchester. During the French and Indian War, he was colonel in charge of Virginia troops protecting the city against Indian raids. The office he used as his head-quarters still stands today and is now a museum.

During the Civil War, Winchester was the scene of savage battles, changing hands 70 or more times during the struggle, and once shifting sides 13 times in a single day. Stonewall Jackson had his headquarters here during the winter of 1861–62; his home is open to the public.

Today Winchester is known as the "Apple Capital of the World," with millions of barrels of apples harvested annually and the world's largest apple cold-storage plant located in Frederick County. In early May, the city is the site of the famous Shenandoah Valley Apple Blossom Festival, an annual event attracting thousands of visitors. There are parades, band contests, arts and crafts displays, and food booths, with the festivities presided over by the year's reigning queen.

A variety of tours are available. For more information, write: Winchester-Frederick County Visitor Center, 1360 S. Pleasant Valley Rd., Winchester, VA 22601, or phone (703) 662-4118.

Abram's Delight (1340 S. Pleasant Valley Rd.). The oldest house in Winchester, Abram's Delight was built in 1754 by Abraham Hollingsworth, an early settler. A yellow balloon-back rocker and fireplace andirons in the shape of Hessian soldiers set the tone of the quaint and cheerful 18th-century-style furnishings in the two floors of the home. Outside in the boxwood garden is a completely and authentically furnished log cabin.

Open daily April through October. Admission charge.

Christ Episcopal Church (Washington Street). A small cemetery adjacent to this 1828 church holds the tomb of Thomas, Lord Fairfax, who lived in the Winchester area from 1748 to 1783. Fairfax, a close friend of young George Washington, was the original proprietor of five million acres in Northern Virginia.

Stonewall Jackson's Headquarters (415 N. Braddock St.). General Jackson made his home and headquarters here from November 1861 to March 1862. Letters to his wife indicate that he was very fond of this house. The study contains the desk he built himself from old barn timbers, and the wallpaper, which he greatly admired, has been reproduced exactly. General Eisenhower, a great fan of Jackson's, donated a German Luger pistol to the museum.

Open daily April through October. Admission charge.

Old Stone Presbyterian Church (306 E. Piccadilly St.). This restored 1788 church was used as a stable for horses by Federal troops during the Civil War, and later as a public school and armory.

Open, free, daily 7 A.M. to 8 P.M.

Washington's Office and Museum (Cork and Braddock streets). Lieut. Col. George Washington, then in command of the Virginia frontier, had his office here from 1756 to 1757 while he was surveying for Lord Fairfax and supervising the erection of Fort Loudoun. A parchment deed signed by Fairfax and a mallet Washington used while surveying to drive stakes and pegs are on display.

The main room contains a closet with a concealed trapdoor leading to an attic. During the Civil War, Confederate soldiers were hidden away here by the townspeople. In an adjoining room, used as a kitchen during the Revolutionary War, bloodstains on the floor can still be seen where the room served as a makeshift Confederate hospital. One especially grim relic is a Confederate saddle. A huge hole shows where a cannonball pierced the soldier's back and his saddle, and even went through to kill the horse.

Open daily April through November. Admission charge.

Woodstock

Massanutten Mountain Observation Tower (4 miles east of Woodstock). This tower affords a panoramic view of seven horseshoe bends of the Shenandoah River in the valley below.

Shenandoah Valley Music Festival (at Pavillion in Orkney Springs). Each March through September, musicians gather here to give symphonic and popular concerts. Arts and crafts shows. For information, write: Manager, Shenandoah Valley Music Festival, P.O. Box 12, Woodstock, VA 22664, or phone (703) 459-3396.

Shenandoah Vineyards (south of Woodstock on U.S. 11, right on VA 605, left on VA 686). Tours and tastings are available at this Shenandoah Valley winery.

Open free daily. Closed Easter, Thanksgiving, Christmas, and New Year's Day.

Wytheville

Valuable lead and salt mines made Wytheville strategically important to both sides during the Civil War, with numerous Federal attempts made to capture the town. The famous 40-mile ride by Molly Tynes prevented a detachment of Union Cavalry from grabbing the prize when she alerted the Confederate guard to come to its defense.

Big Walker Lookout (12 miles north of Wytheville on U.S. 21, 52). A chair-lift ride leads up to an observation tower at an elevation of more than 3,000 feet, with a panoramic view of five states. Hewn-timbered, chestnut-paneled shops are filled with native crafts and gifts from around the world.

Operates daily in summer and weekends in spring and fall. Fee.

Shot Tower Historical State Park (6 miles east of Wytheville on I-81, then 7 miles south on U.S. 52). In 1807 Thomas Jackson, a joint owner of the Lead Mines in Austinville, Virginia, built this 70-foot-high stone tower. Mined lead was carried up the tower's winding stairway to a room where it was placed in a large kettle and heated over a fireplace. When it reached the molten stage, the lead was poured through sieves with holes of varying sizes. The falling drops plunged the 70-foot length of the tower—plus another 75 feet through a shaft sunk beneath the bottom of the floor—before landing in a large kettle of cold water. Well-shaped globular drops formed by the descent rolled into a receptacle, where they were collected and sold as buckshot to hunters. Faulty pellets zigzagged off the incline and were remelted.

Open daily Memorial Day through Labor Day; weekends May and early September through October. Admission charge. Visitor Center, picnic area, walking trails.

Wytheville National Fish Hatchery (12 miles southeast of Wytheville on I-81, U.S. 52, VA 629). Rainbow trout are produced at this hatchery, which also has an aquarium and displays.
Free; open daily 8 to 4.

Yorktown

The town of York was founded in 1691 with the building of a port here. Good harbor facilities made the city one of the major shipping centers in the Chesapeake Bay region throughout the 18th century. When the tobacco trade began to decline, however, the port began to lose its importance, and so did the city, which had depended upon the trade for its prosperity.

Yorktown is best remembered for its role in the American War for Independence, which began at Breed's Hill in 1775 and culminated in the battle fought at Yorktown in 1781. American defeats were common in the early stages of the war, but under the inspired leadership of George Washington—and with the generous aid of France—the tide of battle began to turn in favor of the Americans. When Washington learned in 1781 that Cornwallis was establishing a sea base and making winter quarters at Yorktown, he secretly began to move his combined American and French forces around the town. The French fleet placed a blockade around the British in the harbor, while Washington's troops began a siege on land. The embattled British held on for two weeks, but, outmanned and outgunned, they finally signed the terms of surrender at the Augustine Moore House on October 18, 1781. Total American losses during the Revolution were 4,435.

Yorktown was under siege again in 1862, during the Civil War. Confederate General Magruder used the remains of the Revolutionary War fortifications to set up a defense line against Union General McClellan, who was waging a campaign from Fort Monroe and Newport News against the capital of the Confederacy at Richmond. The Confederates held from April 5 to May 4, 1862, but were driven back under heavy fire, and Union forces were allowed to occupy the town.

Yorktown Battlefield Tour and Visitor Center (end of Colonial Parkway). An introductory film and exhibits give information about the siege, with free maps available for the self-guided auto tour. Markers along the drive also provide information at convenient turnouts. Highlights of the tour include military earthworks, old artillery in position, troop encampments, and the Yorktown National Civil War Cemetery. The terms of the surrender were drafted and signed at the Moore House on October 18, 1781.

Visitor Center open daily, free, 8:30 to 6 Memorial Day through Labor Day, 8:30 to 5 during the rest of the year. Closed Christmas.

Moore House (1 mile east on VA 238). Free; open daily Memorial Day through Labor Day.

Yorktown Victory Center (1/2 mile west of Yorktown on VA 238). Gallery exhibits, multimedia presentations, and a documentary film, *The Road to Yorktown,* shown continuously in the museum theatre, tell the story of America's fight for freedom in the American Revolution. Visitors may stroll down the re-creation of an 18th-century lane and experience the sights and sounds that bring to life the struggle that was raging more than 200 years ago. Outside is an 18th-century military encampment where costumed soldiers relate stories of camp life.

Open daily 9 to 5. Extended hours during the summer. Closed Christmas and New Year's Day. Admission charge. Restaurant.

Although many of Yorktown's oldest homes are closed to the public, scenic surroundings make for a pleasant and informative walking tour. Near Cornwallis Cave there is a small park offering picnic facilities on the banks of the York River, a sandy beach for sunbathing, and dining and overnight accommodations.

Captain John Ballard House (Nelson Street). Built in the early 18th century, this house belonged to a prosperous trade merchant. Private, not open to the public.

Cornwallis Cave (on the York waterfront). A taped narrative at the cave's entrance gives its history. The cave was used by General Cornwallis and his army during the siege of Yorktown, and by Confederate soldiers in 1862.

Free; open daily.

Customhouse (Main and Read streets). Originally a storehouse, this 18th-century building was built by a merchant, who was also the official cargo inspector for the colony.

Dudley Digges House (Main Street). This 1755 house (a restoration) was built by the Comptroller of Customs at Yorktown and Rector of the College of William and Mary. Private, not open to the public.

Grace Episcopal Church (Church Street, near the York River). Built in 1697, the church was completely destroyed by a fire in 1814; it was rebuilt in 1926. The British stored gunpowder and ammunition here during the Revolutionary War, and during the Civil War the building served as a temporary hospital. It is still an active church and contains its original communion silver, made in England in 1649. Thomas Nelson, Jr., signer of the Declaration of Independence, lies buried in the adjacent churchyard.

Church open, free, daily 9 to 5.

Medical Shop (Main Street, next to Courthouse). This building was reconstructed near the medicinal shop built by Dr. Griffin in 1773. The original structure burned in 1814. Private, not open to the public.

Nelson House (Main and Nelson streets). This imposing home, built in 1711, was owned by Thomas Nelson, one of the signers of the Declaration of Independence and a commanding general of the Virginia Militia during the Revolutionary War. General Cornwallis used the house as his headquarters for a short time, and two cannonballs from the bombardment of Yorktown are still embedded in the brick walls. Property of the National Park Service.

145

Open free daily Memorial Day through Labor Day; weekends Easter to Memorial Day and Labor Day through October.

Thomas Pate House (corner of Main and Read streets). Thomas Pate, ferryman and tavern keeper, built this house on a lot he purchased in 1699. Private, not open to the public.

Thomas Sessions House (corner of Main and Nelson streets). This is the oldest house in Yorktown, built about 1692. It was used as headquarters by General T. S. Negly of General McClellan's staff during the Civil War. Private, not open to the public.

Edmund Smith House (Nelson Street). The house was constructed in 1750, and appears today almost exactly as it did then. Private, not open to the public.

Mungo Somerwell House (corner of Main and Church streets). Built in the early 18th century by the ferryman at Yorktown, this building also served as a tavern and ordinary; it was used as a Union hospital during the Civil War. Private, not open to the public.

Swan Tavern (corner of Main and Ballard streets). Now an antique shop; the original tavern building was destroyed by an explosion in 1863.

York County Courthouse (Main and Ballard streets). In 1730 the town raised tobacco to pay for the construction of a new courthouse, built to replace the smaller 1697 building on the same site. The new courthouse was converted to a hospital for the French wounded during the Revolutionary War; after the war it was returned to its former use. In 1814 the structure was destroyed by fire, and it was rebuilt four years later. The courthouse was again destroyed when gunpowder that had been stored inside exploded in December of 1863, setting off a fire that burned down most of the town. Another building was erected some ten years later. It was replaced by the present structure in 1955. Records here date back to 1633.

Open free, 9 to 5, Monday through Friday. Closed holidays.

Yorktown Victory Monument (Main Street). This 95-foot granite column memorializes the surrender of Cornwallis's British forces to Washington at Yorktown. The monument was authorized by Congress ten days after the surrender of Cornwallis, but was not built until 1884. The Goddess of Victory topping the column was sculpted in 1956 to replace one struck by lightning in 1942.

The monument was also erected in recognition of the French contribution to American independence. The French Treasury spent $772 million and had 5,040 battle casualties while supporting the American fight for independence.

Additional
Visitor Information

Camping

Virginia has more than 250 camping facilities from the mountains to the sea in its scenic national parks, 20 state parks, and numerous natural areas and historical parks.

Camping rates and reservation forms may be obtained by writing to: Virginia Ticketron Reservation Center, Box 62221, Virginia Beach, VA 23462; or the Virginia Division of Parks and Recreation, 1201 Washington Building, Capitol Square, Richmond, VA 23219, phone (804) 786-2134. Information booklets are available from the Division of Parks and Recreation, and a campground directory may be obtained from the Virginia Division of Tourism, Bell Tower on Capitol Square, 101 N. Ninth St., Richmond, VA 23219; phone (804) 786-4484.

Fishing

An annual Salt Water Fishing Tournament is held May through November. For tournament information, write: Claude Rogers, Director, Virginia Salt Water Sports Fishing Tournament, Suite 102, Hauser Building, 968 Oriole Dr. S., Virginia Beach, VA 23451, or phone (804) 428-4360. There is no closed season for saltwater fishing and no license is necessary. For other information, write: Virginia Division of Tourism, 101 N. Ninth St., Suite 200, Richmond, VA 23219.

Freshwater fishing is available in a number of lakes and streams in the national and state parks and in the two national forests. For license and fee regulations, write: Commission of Game and Inland Fisheries, Box 11104, Richmond, VA 23230.

Golfing

Virginia offers some of the finest golfing in the country. Resorts offer overnight accommodations, fine dining, other recreation facilities, and some have their own airports for private planes. For a complete listing of courses, including location, phone number, holes and pars, course description, and facilities, write: Virginia Division of Tourism, 101 N. Ninth St., Suite 200, Richmond, VA 23219.

Hunting

Hunting in Virginia is for upland game and waterfowl in season. For license and fee regulations, write the Commission of Game and Inland Fisheries, Box 11104, Richmond, VA 23230.

Skiing

Virginia offers snow-covered slopes, professional ski instruction, rental shops, and complete ski packages. Accommodations range from beautiful mountainside chalets right on the slopes to comfortable village farmhouses with kitchens and fireplaces. Write or phone these popular ski resort areas (some are open year round, with summer resort facilities) for more information:

Bryce Resort, Basye, VA 22810; phone (703) 856-2121.

Homestead Resort, Hot Springs, VA 24445; phone (703) 839-5079.

Massanutten Village Ski Resort, McGaheysville, VA 22840; phone (703) 289-9441.

Wintergreen, Wintergreen, VA 22938; phone (804) 325-2200.

Virginia Division of Tourism

Conveniently located stations operated by the Virginia Division of Tourism provide assistance and free information on travel throughout the state. Counselors will assist in arranging travel itineraries, marking tour routings on free state highway maps, and providing a variety of helpful travel tips. Ten highway travel information stations are located at key rest areas near state lines and remain open seven days a week:

> Interstate 85 near Bracey
> Interstate 81 near Clear Brook
> Interstate 81 near Bristol
> Interstate 95 near Skippers
> Interstate 95 near Fredericksburg
> Interstate 64 near Covington
> Interstate 66 near Manassas
> U.S. 13 on the Eastern Shore
>   near New Church
> Interstate 77 near Lambsburg
> Interstate 77 near Rocky Gap

Prospective visitors may also obtain free travel information and a state map by writing: Virginia Department of Transportation, 1401 E. Broad St., Richmond, VA 23219. For brochures and maps, write: Travel Development Department, Virginia State Chamber of Commerce, 9 S. Fifth St., Richmond, VA 23219. For recreational and tourist information, write: Virginia Division of Tourism, Bell Tower on Capitol Square, 101 N. Ninth St., Richmond, VA 23219, or phone (804) 786-4484.

Annual Calendar of Events

FEBRUARY

ALEXANDRIA: George Washington Birthday Celebrations; George Washington Birthday Parade
WILLIAMSBURG: Antiques Forum; Washington's Birthday Holidays; Colonial Weekends

MARCH

CHINCOTEAGUE: Easter Decoy Festival
MONTEREY: Highland Maple Festival
MOUNT VERNON: Needlework Exhibit, Woodlawn Plantation
WILLIAMSBURG: Canada Time in Williamsburg

APRIL

STATEWIDE HISTORIC GARDEN WEEK IN VIRGINIA
ALEXANDRIA: House Tours; Historic Garden Week
ARLINGTON: Easter Sunrise Services (Arlington National Cemetery)
CHARLOTTESVILLE: Dogwood Festival; Founder's Day (Jefferson's Birthday); Historic Garden Week
FORT MONROE: Easter Sunrise Services
FREDERICKSBURG: Historic Garden Week
FRONT ROYAL: Warren County Garden Tour
GALAX: Blue Ridge Horse Show
HOPEWELL: Prince George Heritage Fair
LEESBURG: Virginia Foxhound Show; Homes and Gardens Tour; Morven Park International Equestrian Institute Horse Trials
LEXINGTON: Garden Week in Historic Lexington
NORFOLK: International Azalea Festival; British Isles Festival

PORTSMOUTH: Pilgrimage to Cape Henry
VINTON: Dogwood Festival Week
WILLIAMSBURG: Historic Garden Week

MAY

STATEWIDE SALT WATER FISHING TOURNAMENT
ABINGDON: Spring Sampler
ARLINGTON: Memorial Day Parade and Services
CHINCOTEAGUE: Seafood Festival
FAIRFAX: Plantation Days
FREDERICKSBURG: Market Square Fair
HARRISONBURG: Virginia Poultry Festival
JAMESTOWN: Settlement Celebration
NEW MARKET: Reenactment of the Battle of New Market
ROANOKE: Festival in the Park; Chili Cookoff
SHENANDOAH: Shenandoah Spring Festival
WILLIAMSBURG: Prelude to Independence
WINCHESTER: Shenandoah Apple Blossom Festival
WYTHEVILLE: Southwest Virginia Horse Show

JUNE

ALEXANDRIA: Red Cross Waterfront Festival
COLONIAL BEACH: Potomac River Festival
FAIRFAX: Antique Car Show
HAMPTON: Hampton Jazz Festival; Hampton Cup Regatta
KILMARNOCK: "A Day for the Arts"
NEWPORT NEWS: Spring Art Show; The Spring Thing
NORFOLK: Harborfest
PORTSMOUTH: Historic Homes Tour
RICHMOND: June Jubilee
ROANOKE: Festival on the River
UPPERVILLE: Colt and Horse Show
VIRGINIA BEACH: Boardwalk Art Show
WILLIAMSBURG: Prelude to Independence
WOODSTOCK: Court Days

JULY

ALEXANDRIA: Virginia Scottish Games; Battle of Fort Stevens
BRISTOL: Carter Family Memorial Festival
CHINCOTEAGUE: Pony Penning
COLONIAL BEACH: Annual Chicken Bar-B-Que
STAUNTON: Happy Birthday USA
SURRY (Chippokes Plantation State Park): Pork, Peanut, and Pine Festival
WILLIAMSBURG: Prelude to Independence

AUGUST

ABINGDON: Virginia Highlands Festival
ARLINGTON: Arlington County Fair
COLONIAL BEACH: Boardwalk Art and Craft Show
DUBLIN (Claytor Lake State Park): Virginia Mountain Crafts Guild Fair
FAIRFAX: Quilt Show
FRONT ROYAL: Warren County Fair; Middleburg Wine Festival and Vineyard Tour
GALAX: Old Fiddler's Convention
HARRISONBURG: Natural Chimneys Jousting Tournament
LEESBURG: August Court Days
MANASSAS: Prince William County Fair; Civil War Reenactment
ORANGE: Orange County Street Festival
STAUNTON-AUGUSTA COUNTY: Jousting Tournaments
VIRGINIA BEACH: East Coast Surfing Championship
WOODSTOCK: Shenandoah County Fair

SEPTEMBER

ALEXANDRIA: Hospital Auxiliary Event
DANVILLE: Danville Harvest Jubilee; Annual National Auctioneering Contest
FREDERICKSBURG: Quilt Show
GALAX: Galax-Carroll-Grayson County Fair
HAMPTON: Hampton Bay Days
LORTON: Gunston Hall Car Show
OCCOQUAN: Craft Show
RICHMOND: Virginia State Fair
VIRGINIA BEACH: Neptune Festival
WILLIAMSBURG: Seniors Time; Publick Times

OCTOBER

CHINCOTEAGUE: Oyster Festival
CLIFTON FORGE: Fall Festival
FRONT ROYAL: Festival of Leaves
LURAY: Page County Heritage Festival
MARTINSVILLE: Blue Ridge Folklife Festival
NEWPORT NEWS: Fall Festival
PETERSBURG: Nostalgiafest
RICHMOND: Richmond Newspapers Marathon
WAYNESBORO: Fall Foliage Festival
YORKTOWN: "Celebration of Victory"

NOVEMBER

ALEXANDRIA: Washington's Review of the Troops

CHARLES CITY (Berkeley Plantation): Virginia Thanksgiving Celebration
CHINCOTEAGUE: Water Fowl Week
LEESBURG: Christmas at Oatlands
LURAY: Christmas in Luray
RICHMOND: First Thanksgiving Berkeley Plantation
ROANOKE: Crafts Festival
URBANNA: Oyster Festival

DECEMBER

ALEXANDRIA: Scottish Christmas Walk
FREDERICKSBURG: Christmas Candlelight Tour
LEXINGTON: "Holiday in Lexington"
LORTON (Gunston Hall): Carols by Candlelight
RICHMOND: Christmas Open House Tour
WILLIAMSBURG (COLONIAL WILLIAMSBURG): Grand Illumination

Each year dozens of events open to the public are held throughout the state. Because the events are subject to cancellation without notice and because the dates vary, it is best to contact the sponsors directly before beginning your trip in order to avoid disappointment.

A complete yearly calendar of events with sponsors' addresses and telephone numbers may be obtained by writing to the Travel Development Department, Virginia State Chamber of Commerce, 9 S. Fifth St., Richmond, VA 23219.

Index

Printed in the United States
64688LVS00002B/934-957

9 780882 897325